)

That Strange Divine Sea

CHRISTOPHER DERRICK

That Strange Divine Sea

Reflections on Being a Catholic

IGNATIUS PRESS   SAN FRANCISCO

With ecclesiastical approval
© Ignatius Press 1983
All rights reserved
ISBN 0–89870–029–9
Library of Congress Catalogue number 83–080190
Printed in the United States of America

Contents

Introduction

The purpose and method of this book call for a little explanation: otherwise, the reader may start off on the wrong foot and with expectations of the wrong sort. My title is stolen from another writer and may be allowed to remain enigmatic for the time being. But my subtitle should be noted. These are not the reflections of a saint or even a theologian: this is not a helpful work of devotion and spirituality, or an outline of Catholic belief, or a robustly controversial apologetic. I offer nothing more than one man's reflections upon his own experience of 'being a Catholic'—and not a particularly good Catholic—throughout a mostly fortunate lifetime, and in particular through the changes and confusions of these last few years.

I hope thereby to cast a little light upon something which, for many people, has been thrown into considerable obscurity by those changes and confusions—the *meaning* of 'being a Catholic', in the sense of its point or value or importance or (the popularity of this jargon-word is significant) its 'relevance'.

This is a highly personal book: I offer only one man's reflections upon that subject. The pronoun 'I' recurs in these pages with a frequency that may well suggest self-centredness, perhaps with good cause: if given its head, this book would have become a kind of auto-biography. Then, its literary method (or lack of method) is very unlike what I would have chosen for an attempt to expound and explain and prove something. The intellect is the organ of truth, but the imagination is the organ of meaning: I here address the imagination much more than the intellect, and therefore make more use of image and analogy and anecdote and quotation than of reasoned argument. "We make out of the quarrel with others, rhetoric", said Yeats, "but of the quarrel with ourselves, poetry." I am already guilty of controversial rhetoric in amply sufficient quantity: what follows is at least relatively close to poetry, in the limited sense of exploring certain experiences and thoughts and meanings, as encountered by me in the course of my long quarrel with myself and God, and in the further sense of suggesting certain modes of feeling and lines of thought rather than following them out in any systematic way.

Suggestion and a lack of system, even of continuity—that's what you must expect to find in this *causerie*, this set of *pensées*. In the ninth century Nennius assembled a great rag-bag of history and legend and said of it most proudly, "*Coacervavi omne quod inveni*", "I made a heap of everything I could find", and David Jones cited this precedent for his deeply Catholic rag-bag of a poem *The Anathemata*, which he subtitled "Fragments of an Attempted Writing". That is very much the spirit in which I proceed, offering (in a way) nothing but sweepings and left-overs. Granite chips litter the floor of a sculptor's studio, wood shavings litter the floor of a carpenter's workshop: these are the sweepings of a literary and controversial mind, accumulated over many years and now arranged in a very rough kind of order. They bear the marks of their origin, and the reader will detect many echoes of current or recent controversy among them. But they are not here offered controversially. If at times I appear to be arguing, I'm mostly arguing with myself. These sweepings also bear the marks of my twofold fixation upon words and (more absurdly) upon aircraft and flying.

Diagnosis comes before treatment, question comes before answer; and so, before offering my reflections upon being a Catholic, I offer certain reflections upon *not* being a Catholic. I consider the human problem first of all, and only then, some aspects of what I take to be God's answer to that problem. (Some aspects, not all. I operate selectively, with a certain concentration upon sensitive areas and with no attempt to cover the entire ground. You will find this book electrifying in the scope and scale of its omissions.) In between and a shade more systematically—a shade more controversially too—I attempt a little semantic repair-work upon the three key words: 'Christian', 'Church', and 'Catholic'. For the obscurity into which the concept of 'being a Catholic' has now been thrown for so many, the blurred and broken condition of those key words is partly to blame.

Chapter One

The Raw Human Condition

"The mass of men lead lives of quiet desperation", said Thoreau.

Do they indeed? There is certainly a great deal of suffering in this world. But humanity has always been able to cope with the chronic imperfection of life—sometimes by apathy, sometimes by resigned fortitude, sometimes by aspiring to a less imperfect future, and often by retreat into some inward vision or hope.

Perhaps 'desperation' is too strong a word. Could that be anybody's *permanent* condition? To me it suggests a kind of crisis, a moment when things suddenly become unendurable for a period that cannot possibly be extended: there has to be some early resolution, even if it is only the resolution of death.

And if you look around and observe your fellowmen—on some bright spring morning, here in one of the wealthier countries and in congenial surroundings—you may well feel that Thoreau's words are altogether too gloomy. How brightly and cheerfully people go about their affairs! How actively occupied they are, how purposeful! How many smiling faces you see, how much casual laughter you hear! True, we all have our troubles and problems. But most people appear to rub along contentedly enough if not always joyfully, having their black moments but taking the rough with the smooth: 'desperation' is surely a rare thing.

The psychiatrist or the social worker might tell you a different story: also the doctor, and of course the priest.

One thing has long seemed clear to me. When not enjoying their leisure, people commonly do present an appearance of being busily, actively, and purposefully occupied; and each one, if asked, could tell you how important his activities were. But such assertions are seldom to be taken at their face value. We certainly do many things because they need to be done. But we also do them because we need to do *something*: it is not only for economic reasons that we look with horror upon any prospect of unemployment, despite its partial resemblance to leisure, a thing which we all enjoy. Hence the politicians can speak of 'job-creation' as a desirable thing, despite the implied reversal of means and ends. The point isn't only that certain tasks need to be done and that men must therefore be set to work: it's also that men cannot endure to be unoccupied for long and must therefore be given something to do, no matter how fatuous and footling it is when considered objectively and on its merits, no matter how irrelevant to every real human need except that need to be busy.

So we cause life to be filled with a fume and fret of activity, largely pointless in itself and sometimes pernicious. The poets and saints urge us to refrain from all that and to live more simply, more contemplatively: are they aware of the cost and the danger?

> What is this life if, full of care,
> We have no time to stand and stare?

But what if we *did* stand and stare, what if we "saw life steadily and saw it whole", and so perceived nothing but emptiness and unmeaning and demons, and the great grin of forthcoming Death?

"That way madness lies." No wonder we keep ourselves busy and full of care, as though in mere self-preservation: to be unoccupied is to be alone with one's self and the universe and the absurdity of our condition, and so to be filled with existential dread. "I believe that most of human activity", said T. F. Powys, "particularly work of the mechanical, non-creative sort, is Man's invention to avoid the terror of contemplation."

There are of course further ways of avoiding that terror. There's sociability and casual chatter, for example, and equally casual reading; there's sport, there's fun and games, there are hobbies; there are such drugs as tobacco and the demon drink and (of course) television. Such things soften the impact of primary experience, and who can blame the addict? As Scott observed, "Life could not be endured were it seen in reality."

All men know this, even those who strike us as being extroverted and cheerful and carefree, confidently engaged with this or that, untroubled by the tragedy and despair of the raw human condition. We should not be deceived by social appearances, by the brave act put on by such people when in public.

An act is what it is, made easier by distractions. What is really in the mind of each when he lies awake at three in the morning? when, alone, he remembers his childhood and wonders about his death?

When I was a boy, I often used to go cycling around the Wiltshire Downs, those great uplands of grass and wind, contrasting most starkly with the leafy cosiness that elsewhere characterises southern England.

Neolithic man has left his mark everywhere in those

uplands. Stonehenge is of course well known, Silbury Hill and Avebury rather less so: I used to contemplate those haunted places in deep amazement, also the un-numbered barrows and tumuli that dot the high severe landscape.

The imagination races in such surroundings, helped along by one's archaeological reading and by fictional interpretations as well: one tries to envisage those strange people of the remote past, our ancestors yet so unlike ourselves.

The past? Yes; but, although this obvious fact is always hard to take in, it wasn't a past while it was going on. It was Neolithic man's Today, his Now. How did he experience it? Did his people "lead lives of quiet desperation"? One tries to imagine their existence, their daily routine: the shivering, the skins, the raw meat, the weapons and implements of flint: "No arts; no letters, no society; and which is worst of all, continual fear and danger of violent death; and the life of man, solitary, poor, nasty, brutish, and short."

So we like to envisage it, anyway, since doctrines of Progress are flattering to ourselves—even though com-parable primitives, recently surviving in remote places, have seldom seemed as miserable as all that. We know, of course, that if catapulted back by magic into that Neolithic condition, we would be unable to cope and so in desperation. But isn't that very much what they would feel too, if magically catapulted forward into present-day London or New York? Wouldn't they then suppose themselves to be in some abode of madness and demons, some kind of Hell?

Perhaps 'happiness'—in some senses of the word— is very much a matter of what one is used to, and 'desperation' a matter of the unmanageably strange and new. Bad news if so: death, if an experience at all, will then be an experience of total desperation. But this can't be the whole story, since we are so often bored to tears by the over-familiar.

How absolute are such contrasts, anyway? It is so easy to be bemused by all these jets and cars and computers, and to forget that we are only what men always were, inescapably stuck in the raw human condition, although some of us are at present insulated from some of its hardships. The sun still rises over those Wiltshire Downs very much as it did when the pattern of its rising prompted the unimaginable building of Stonehenge: we are still only men, creeping about on the surface of the same planet, still members of the same species as those Neolithic people and—if it comes to that—as the Bushmen of the Kalahari and the Eskimos and the aborigines of the Gibson Desert. Like all these, we are born of woman: we grow up, we struggle for a living, we live individually but socially too; we mate and reproduce our kind; we do not suffer all the time but we always suffer; we are haunted by mystery, we feel that we have offended the gods and therefore try to placate their anger; we die.

That last statement is about as uncontroversial as it could be, however hard to take in so far as one's own case is concerned. I sometimes look steadily at my left hand and try to imagine it becoming the hand of a corpse, as I suppose it will before long. But it's hard to believe. Will I really spend years and centuries gazing up at the lid of a wooden box? Or will I perhaps end up as a crisp radio-active cinder, bowling along in the light breezes of an empty world?

Either way, how can 'I' be the one who does so?

However that may be, the fact seems clear. The blood of my Neolithic kinsmen is long dried up in those barrows and tumuli: it runs in my veins, but—as in theirs—only for a time.

"For want of me the world's course will not fail"; and of course I shall live on in my children and grand-children, unless some nuclear holocaust does indeed put an end to us all.

We have often been told that it may do so; and this makes us feel distinctly helpless, since we simply do not know what political and other developments will either increase or diminish the likelihood of that Final Solution. Some of us agonise a great deal over this question, which is very understandable: the trouble is that we can thereby be distracted from the fact that our human condition always was a temporary thing. Let all weapons of mass destruction be annihilated by magic, let all the problems of poverty and injustice and suffering be miraculously resolved: if only for astronomical reasons, it will still remain true that our planet cannot support human life for ever. Our collective story, like each individual's story, ends in death.

Do we need to worry about this? I suppose we ought to be concerned for the long-term future of humanity. But I, at least, am not. However shameful the confession may be, I don't really care twopence about what the state of mankind will be in five hundred years' time. I care passionately about my children, slightly less about my grandchildren, and I will probably care rather less still about my great-grandchildren, should I ever see them: I find my present concern diminishing geometrically from one future generation to another.

It's in quite a different sense that I'm bothered by the fact of our collective mortality: even more than one's personal mortality, it draws attention to the seeming *pointlessness* of our existence in this world.

There's an old joke about this. "I know what I am here for: I was put into the world in order to care for others. But what are the others for?"

We live for the future, say; we hope to leave this world a better place than we found it. Each one of us may perhaps be able to do that, up to a point and on however small a scale. He can at least refrain from making it a worse world. But the psychology of all such attempts must suffer a distinct shock when we remember that in the long term, and perhaps in the short term, the human future is a lost cause. There's less and less of it as every day goes by, and more and more of the past. If we live for the future we serve a dying god, and one with little prospect of rising again.

Another old joke: in our exertions to remedy the human condition, we are only re-arranging the deck-chairs on the sinking *Titanic*.

Well, it is no bad thing for deck-chairs to be arranged as well as possible, whatever the circumstances. The temporary is not automatically the pointless. We can enjoy a holiday despite its brief duration, and doctors try to prolong life while knowing that they cannot make men immortal. Only a very poor-spirited fellow would argue that, because we cannot make everything perfect and permanent, we should sit back in despair and neglect such limited hopes and temporary improvements as do lie within our reach.

The ship is sinking, even so; and the remembered fact of death, both individual and collective, confronts us with the mystery of our being—its existential absurdity—

even as we work on the deck-chairs. One's own mortality is the most insane fact of all. How can anything be so totally inevitable and yet so totally unimaginable?

One thinks of it with a kind of fascination. Which of us has never imagined himself as being under sentence of death? as sitting there in the condemned cell, smoking and reading and passing the time generally, and knowing that this coming Tuesday (unlike the others) will not be followed by a Wednesday?

We all live on Death Row in fact, though with the execution-date concealed from most of us. But do we really *believe* in this absurd happening?

Death is something that happens to other people.

But suffering is something that happens to oneself.

It also happens to others, of course, and on lines that hardly bear consideration. I write these words on a summer morning of sunshine and flowers and birdsong; and in this morning's paper, I read of a man whose son was killed in a motorcycle accident. He went off to the funeral, and when he came home afterwards, they told him that he had also lost two daughters and three grandchildren in an airline disaster.

What can possibly be said about a happening like that, or about the totality of human pain and misery and grief?

There is some comfort, perhaps, in the fact that nobody experiences that totality. Individuals suffer in their varying degrees and in some cases, no doubt, up to the very limit of what human nature can endure. Let us suppose that a million people are now suffering at that extreme intensity: even then, suffering at a million times that intensity will not be taking place anywhere.

Cold comfort.

In itself, suffering is not wholly unmanageable. The cardinal virtue of Fortitude cannot be very difficult, since it appears to be sufficiently well mastered by any number of ordinary people, not only by rare saints and heroes; and there are of course some who get through life on remarkably easy terms, without needing very much of that virtue.

I haven't got very much of it myself. I simply hate suffering: that is to say, I hate everything that conflicts with my own will. The great though limited wisdom of the Buddhists might be relevant in such a case. If I ceased to will, to wish, to want, to desire, I would doubtlessly cease to suffer.

But I find something inhuman in the very idea of ceasing to suffer on those terms. Think of that man who suffered a sixfold bereavement within a few days. It is conceivable that, before the event, he might have attained perfection in Buddhist tranquillity, in Stoic *apatheia*, and might so have been unmoved by this frightful blow of fate. Conceivable, yes; but desirable? In that case, wouldn't he be something less than a man?

The blows of fate, more or less frightful, come upon all of us sooner or later, and they hurt. We are a tough resilient species, of course, and it is amazing how quickly and completely some people recover from those blows at their worst, retaining their sanity and even a kind of cheerfulness. Others get permanently broken.

This aspect of the raw human condition makes for despair—not because of suffering itself, but because of its seeming pointlessness, its random distribution. Why do some people suffer so very much more than others? If this was always because of wickedness—in themselves or even in others—we might claim to see a pattern and even a point. But it isn't; nor can we say, in any sweeping fashion, that suffering purifies the soul and improves the character. If it makes for holiness in one man, it makes for venomous bitterness in another.

Why shouldn't we curse God for all this, if there is a God?

It's all in the Book of Job. Job did curse God, having been very badly treated, and God doesn't appear to have minded. But he did offer a reply—one which, if stripped of its tremendous poetry and put into the jargon of our time, would amount to "It is neither morally proper nor logically coherent for a creature to sit in judgment upon his Creator."

A sufficient reply?

The story does have a happy ending: Job is restored to something better than his original condition. But why couldn't he have been left as he was from the start?

It wasn't as if he was a *wicked* man, after all.

The fact of death sets a time-limit to even the best of our temporal hopes: the fact of suffering limits their effective plausibility. We 'hope for the best', as the gloomy saying goes, but we hardly expect it: we know that things are not likely to go uniformly and universally well in this life, whatever form the future may take. Things can be expected to go fairly well, for some people and up to a point and for a time. Then Fortune gives her roulette-wheel another spin.

We suffer and we die. The fact also needs to be faced that we are sinners, wicked people, and—so long as our condition remains raw—*unforgivably* so, in the most literal sense of that adverb.

It was once normal for people to be painfully aware of this fact. Bunyan could represent Christian as bowed down by an intolerable burden of guilt: primitive and pagan religions have always made the easing of such burdens into a primary concern: Jesus, offering forgiveness, could assume a consciousness of personal guilt in his hearers. It would be rash to make any such assumption nowadays. Too many people take it for granted that, where guilt-feelings exist, they always add up to a pathological delusion to be remedied by the analyst, never to a realism about ourselves.

It would be easy to blame modern psychology, or at least, popular misunderstandings of it, for this state of affairs. But that isn't the whole story: other factors have been at work.

For one thing, our age has been remarkably fruitful (if not uniquely so) in spectacular public evil: Auschwitz, Hiroshima, the Gulag Archipelago. This enables us to *distance* the concept of 'wickedness'. You and I naturally have our faults. But a word which is applicable to Himmler and Stalin cannot also be applied to ourselves without absurdity: 'wickedness' then becomes something done—exceptionally—by alien people in remote places.

The media do something similar in respect of those moral evils which are less exceptional and spectacular but still grievous. If we had lived before printing and radio and television, we would only have known about those rapes and murders that took place in our immediate vicinity, and these would have been few in number: now, since 'news' is mostly bad news, we read about such things happening everywhere and all the time. Our catchment-area for such reportage is much wider. This helps us to feel pretty virtuous. We aren't like Himmler and Stalin: we aren't even like the dreadful people you read about in every day's newspapers.

Finally, a prevailing humanism causes us to base our

standards of good and bad behaviour upon what we observe in our fellowmen, upon the generally-accepted standards of the society in which we happen to live. We can thus speak of *ordinary decent people*, not saints but not sinners either, or not in any serious sense; and we can plausibly claim to be included among these. We don't do much that isn't common form. Exceptional wickedness is an exceptional thing, after all: moral normality is normal: the average decent man (such as oneself) is just about as virtuous as the average decent man generally is.

One's conscience can then sleep peacefully, lulled into unconcern by tautologies.

Feelings of personal guilt do continue, and they are sometimes pathological in nature. But they appear to have suffered considerable weakening.

This is not to say that the moral sense has suffered some general attenuation: it's probably as strong as ever it was. But it has been re-directed. Guilt is now attributed much less to the self, much more to others and (conspicuously) to structures and institutions. If some prophet were to appear among us and accuse us all of sin, it would be our instinct to reply, "How right you are!—look at *him*, for example, or *him*! Look at the rotten society we live in!" Only a few would beat their individual breasts.

It is both easy and enjoyable to repent of other people's sins, to apologise to God and man on their behalf. This goes notably for the great public evils, which are mostly committed by other people, only in some minute contributory way by oneself—in one's capacity as a tax-payer, perhaps. They have this further charm as well, that they provide great scope for self-righteous combativeness and aggression, such as we like to justify under the name of 'protest'.

Thus, for a variety of reasons, we have mostly ceased to see our raw condition in terms of personal sin. But we must still concede that, in our collective capacity, we human beings have always behaved culpably and have so made the most frightful mess of things. Our story was always bound to be imperfect, no doubt, and such non-moral factors as madness and misfortune have helped to make it more imperfect than it theoretically needed to be. But how much more has been done by simple wickedness!

History, said Gibbon, is "little more than the register of the crimes, follies, and misfortunes of mankind": he put the crimes first, and we can hardly doubt that many of the follies were culpable. So it was for Rebecca West: "It is often very hard to tell the difference between history and the smell of skunk"—a smell that rises un-abated from the continuing history of our times.

I have heard it argued that there cannot possibly be a just God. If there were, he would have lost patience with us centuries ago. Another Flood? and without a Noah this time?

It isn't easy to see why he holds back.

There are some who, conceding so much, still deny the fact of our individual sin, our personal guilt and need of personal forgiveness, far beyond what we can confer upon one another. But where you find it possible to speak to one of these in his vulnerable loneliness, you will nearly always find that one question gets through his defensive armour and strikes home: "How would you like to get your innocence back, if only you could?"

He may well disbelieve in any possibility of getting it back. But when thus taken by surprise, he will be forced to remember something that he has known for a long time but prefers to forget—the fact that he once had personal innocence but doesn't have it now.

One practical difficulty: he may think that you're referring to sexual innocence alone.

There was once a lady who went to a psychiatrist and said, "Doctor, you've got to help me—I feel so guilty, so hopeless, so terribly *alone*!"

The psychiatrist leaped up and shook her hand warmly. "My dear lady, let me congratulate you! You're the sanest and most realistic person I've met for years! People *are* guilty and hopeless and alone: it's the attempt to pretend otherwise that ties them in psychological knots and makes them profitable to me! No, I won't take a penny: I'm delighted to have met you, good morning."

Every man is an island, entire of itself: even in love, we only meet one another as "ships that pass in the night". Our human experience is of loneliness, of estrangement, of alienation, as though we were strangers and exiles and didn't really belong here. We know that things aren't as good as they might be, and we suffer accordingly. But quite apart from that, we are—in our more honestly thoughtful moments—dimly aware of having lost something undefinable, not to be equated too simply with our lost innocence.

The human animal feels imperfectly at home in any possible environment, even the best that this world can offer. Biologically speaking, we know that we're part of 'Nature': yet we gaze upon it from the outside, as though through an invisible but impermeable sheet of plate glass, envying the other creatures' sense of belonging, of being at home. The 'beauties of Nature'—when Nature *is* beautiful, which isn't always to human eyes—seem like a secret club that we are not allowed to join.

"I cannot get rid of a something that always intrudes between my heart and the blue of every sky", said George MacDonald.

If Original Sin—its consequences, rather—were not a fact of daily experience, half the poets would be out of a job.

The grief of our condition lies partly in the fact that we don't know what it is that we're excluded from, what it is that we want. All manner of short-term satisfactions are available, and most of us secure and enjoy some of them at least. But they leave us still unsatisfied, still inexplicably short of happiness, even when things are at their best. "In sooth, we know not why we are so sad."

What do we really want?

Most of us, if confronted with that question, would laugh uneasily and offer semi-facetious and cynical answers. It's obvious enough what we want! We want lots of money, good health, long life, delicious food and drink, rewarding work or perhaps carefree idleness, splendidly exciting adventures or perhaps nice undemanding tranquillity, home life and beloved children or perhaps a gorgeous freedom from such encumbrances, plenty of sex without any tiresome complications. . . .

Well, all those things and others like them are available and are in fact enjoyed by some. Do they add up to the *whole* of what you want? If you had all of them, exactly as preferred by yourself, would the experience of 'wanting' be absent from your life?

You might well want something else, while feeling shy about mentioning the fact, this further desire being curiously undefinable. Most of us have it, perhaps all of us, but many people repress it into the subconscious— partly because it's painful, and partly because it makes us feel rather foolish. It makes perfect sense to want this or that; but it seems utterly senseless to want. . . ?

To show what I have in mind, let me recall a moment in the emotionally turbulent years of my own adolescence.

Very late on a summer evening, I stood on the ridge of hills that lie above the river Kennet in Berkshire, and I looked westwards. The red afterglow of sunset was barred with purple, and I saw Inkpen Beacon and the hills around it sharply outlined on the horizon.

Now I had often been to those very hills: I had more than once climbed Inkpen Beacon itself, to stare with fascination at the ancient gallows that then stood on its summit. But now, seeing them from afar in the dusk, I found myself consumed by an almost sickening desire to go there again, to *be* there at once, to possess them in some wholly undefinable way. This was utterly unlike the ordinary exploratory urge that had already taken me there in fact. I felt—absurdly—that I was gazing at the Happy Land, the Garden of the Hesperides, the Well at the World's End, the Land of Heart's Desire, with a longing that defies description; and at the same time, I knew perfectly well that I was only looking at some Berkshire hills in the fading light, and that, if I were to go there immediately, they would turn out to be only another place, already known and very pleasant and interesting, but quite incapable of satisfying that desire, that wild longing.

I have sometimes found myself looking back on my country childhood with exactly the same sort of longing. Many others have done so too:

Happy those early days when I
Shin'd in my angel-infancy

—though as we all know, infancy is neither angelic nor uniformly happy. Small children rage and weep and despair quite as much as they ever will in later life, perhaps much more. Childhood is no Paradise Lost. Yet we cannot help remembering it as though it were. Like those hills at dusk, it appears to serve as a kind of metaphor and a powerful one, a pretend-object for piercing desires whose real object—if any—cannot even be imagined.

I sometimes suspect that such hauntings are largely responsible, not only for the grief of our condition, but also for many of our practical follies. People do so many things which they are not obliged to do, and which they do not even *want* to do, or not very seriously: much human behaviour is irrational by any possible standard. How far is this because we find it so painful to face the question of what we really want?

'People don't know what they really want': reverse the grammar of that sentence, and it becomes 'The real object of human desire lies beyond human experience.'

If there is such an object, that is. No doubt the psychologists could explain away these "immortal longings" of ours, probably on sexual lines. They make no sense and get us nowhere: we should ignore them, perhaps, and concentrate upon more substantial matters.

C. S. Lewis is the outstanding writer about this subject, and about the insufficiency of all such brisk dismissals. They don't work. The wound remains, still unhealed and bleeding, however effortfully ignored.

In all that I have said so far, there is absolutely nothing new. Humanity has always known about the grief and despair of its own condition and has come to terms with it in one way or another, commonly by thinking of other things. Most people manage to rub along somehow, without going out of their minds or committing suicide.

But we, in this generation, may find ourselves driven to a relatively new *kind* of despair. Certain temporal hopes, once entertained with great confidence, appear to be losing their plausibility. Until recently, one could look forward to the coming of a better world, and this gave us something to live for: we could be future-oriented, we could live in collective hope and so—to some degree—in individual hope as well. A man knew that he would die one day. But he could believe, with no obvious folly, that his children would live in a better world than his own. Now there is much to suggest that they will live in a nastier and more painful world—if they live at all, that is. As we all know and as I have already observed, *Homo sapiens* has now worked out methods of destroying himself altogether.

Conative behaviour, ordered towards future good of some sort, is of course natural to our species. But one might argue that it was always a folly to be future-oriented in any more general sense. A passage in his *Notebooks* suggests that Leonardo da Vinci had misgivings about all such habits of the mind. "The man who with constant longing awaits with joy each new springtime, each new summer, each new month and year—deeming that the things he longs for are ever too late in coming—does not perceive that he is longing for his own destruction." Impatience for one's future may well be a kind of impatience for death: it might or might not follow that nostalgia is essentially a love of life.

Primitive or traditional peoples were seldom future-oriented. They found life hard but manageable in some fashion, so long as the old traditions and observances were followed precisely, and they expected any radically new happening to be a bad happening—a war, a plague, a famine. But in the West of these last two centuries, this natural conservatism gave place to moods and doctrines of Progress, of an Evolution that went far beyond any theorem in biology, of a Historical Dialectic from which great things could be expected. It thus became possible to trust the future, to live for it. There would always be ups and downs. But generally speaking, one could expect radically new happenings to be improvements. One could live in hope, and many people did.

We find it much harder to do so now, and not simply because we live in fear of a nuclear holocaust. It isn't only on that account that the word 'Progress'—once used in such confidence—can hardly be uttered nowadays without irony.

There are two versions of temporal hope, once powerful but now very much weakened, that call for mention here: also a slightly comical third, more recent in its rise and in its decline as well.

Chesterton once observed that when men cease to believe in God, the trouble is not that they then believe in nothing: it's that they then believe in *anything*. Thus one can easily find people whose parents were believing Christians but who themselves believe in Marxism or astrology or something like that.

People have to believe in *something*, its nature depending upon how they perceive the human condition. In recent decades, post-religious people have shown a marked tendency to see that condition in political terms above all and, hence, to have great faith in politics and political improvement, despite a historical record which hardly warrants such faith.

For my part, while knowing that anarchism is not a real option, I improve upon Karl Marx by saying that politics is the opium of the people. H. L. Mencken came close to the mark when he said that "all government is evil, and that trying to improve it is largely a waste of time". The point is not that such efforts are pernicious in themselves: it is, rather, that their outcome tends to be random in nature, ill-related to whatever good or bad things were intended. "Why, Sir," said Dr. Johnson, "most schemes of political improvement are very laughable things." Sir William Jones pierced to the heart of the matter in that same eighteenth century: "My opinion is that power should always be distrusted, in whatever hands it is placed."

"Put not your trust in princes", says the Good Book. But people had to believe in something; so they clung desperately to the fantasy that while *those* princes were obviously wicked and untrustworthy, *these* princes—the ones on our side—were sound and wise and selfless people who, once in power, could be trusted to devote themselves effectively to 'the common good' and all the other ends of political action as ideally conceived.

It has never worked out like that, and least of all when the chosen means were revolutionary. There are few generalisations that can be made with realism about politics and the historical process, and one of them is this: 'Supposedly liberating revolutions always end up as extremist tyrannies.'

Faith in politics is bad enough: faith in the political Left is even sillier. Yet some people still cling to it, *faute de mieux* and blindly, in the style of those liberal intellectuals who went to see Stalin's Russia and thought they were beholding Paradise. But the timeless gullibility of such people is (or should be) notorious. "Experience beats in vain upon a congenital progressive", said C. S. Lewis.

Every substantial cause, good or bad, has had wicked things done on its behalf. But what cause has ever had more innocent blood on its hands than the cause of the political and revolutionary Left, as existing since the French Revolution?

Yet people still hope and trust in it, precisely— sometimes explicitly—because they must hope and trust in *something*. "To keep hope alive", said Sartre, "one must, in spite of all mistakes, horrors and crimes, recognise the obvious superiority of the Socialist camp."

"*To keep hope alive*"! Desperate words from a prophet of despair.

I speak there, mostly, in the past tense: my experience and reading suggest that a general faith in politics, and in salvation by political methods, is now much less prevalent and powerful than it was in my younger days. It is still powerful, of course, among Socialists and Communists—also, in another version, among Americans. This may be because 'being an American' is an inherently political concept, whereas 'being a Frenchman' (say) is not.

Elsewhere, I think one can detect a gratifying growth of new political cynicism. This does not necessarily prevent people from voting and otherwise being active politically. But it means that they vote and act 'against' rather than 'for'. They see wicked and untrustworthy princes. But reasonably enough, they regard these as preferable to others who seem a great deal worse, and they act accordingly. The idea that we can hope for positively *good* princes—as though wise and virtuous people were ever likely to engage in unscrupulous power-struggles and then to win them—has, I believe, declined considerably in influence; and with it, one sort of temporal optimism.

Another kind of hope for the future has become even more implausible. Where the human condition is not seen in primarily political terms, post-religious man will often see it in primarily economic terms: ever-increasing wealth then becomes the thing that gives hope, the thing that we live for.

That hope, once plausible, now seems rash. Since the 1950s, certain countries have enjoyed a steadily-rising 'standard of living' and have so become more or less 'affluent', a development which came to be seen widely as the destined and permanent order of things, leaving only the question of how to extend it to the poorer countries. Now, however, it seems much more likely to prove a passing phase, a freak of history.

I write at a time of severe world-wide economic recession, and for many, this has just *got* to be a temporary thing; so the politicians—desiring votes, unwilling to say unwelcome things—keep on claiming to see light at the end of the tunnel and telling us that we'll soon be on the economic up-and-up, once again and forever. They then speak in blind faith rather than in any sort of realism: as E. F. Schumacher pointed out, the problem of ever-increasing plenty for all has not been solved and is more than likely to prove insoluble.

We shouldn't grieve too bitterly on that account, since affluence has little to do with happiness and much less to do with the natural and Christian virtues. But many people appear to have become emotionally dependent upon that vision of an ever-richer future, as upon a faith: many Americans, for example, appear to see it as an integral part of the American Dream, so giving it an importance of the quasi-religious kind.

But they are not alone: here in England, too, I have often found it cherished on quasi-religious lines, as constituting the main point and purpose of life. By way of an experiment, I have frequently questioned its plausibility, suggesting—in suitably mixed company—that the days of expansion may be over and that our future is more than likely to be relatively and perhaps permanently poor. When I do, there is invariably someone who cries out as though in despair: "Then what's the good of going on *at all*?"

Men need some kind of faith, some kind of hope. But those who live for a politically or economically better future are courting disappointment and despair. The false gods always break their worshippers' hearts.

They don't always do so immediately: for a time, their worship can seem wondrously supportive. 'Progress and the Golden Future': how comforting it must have been for millions, that fine Victorian confidence, in its capitalist and its Marxist versions equally! It survived, as a mood and to some extent a doctrine, well into my own adult lifetime. But I seldom encounter it now except in a few splendid old diehards. Few of us believe in Brave New Worlds any more: in my experience, most people now greet any mention of 'the future' with a wry grimace. "Well, I hope I don't live to see it."

I am concerned with the raw human condition and—here—with the hopes that once seemed likely to alleviate its tragedy and despair: not with theological controversy. Yet in this present context, I cannot keep silent about a curious revival of very much that same confidence in some of my fellow-Catholics. This follows the Marxist rather than the capitalist pattern, and it has only the flimsiest connection with what Christians have traditionally called the virtue of Hope: it involves vibrantly irrational faith in a recent Revolutionary Moment and in a Brave New Church that is emerging in consequence, so promising us a Golden Future. It's as though we once suffered under the King or Emperor and the Nobles, represented here by the Pope and the Bishops: then came the Storming of the Bastille, represented by the Second Vatican Council as mythologically seen. Thus was freedom established, thus was power transferred—nominally to the Sovereign People, but actually (as in all such cases) to the Party, represented here by a self-appointed élite of the liberal Catholic intelligentsia.

Where this revolution has succeeded (which is far from being everywhere) its consequences have been uniformly disastrous. The Party will never admit this, of course, just as the Party in Moscow will never admit that the Soviet people enjoy anything short of perfect freedom and plenty. But as in Moscow, one has to allow them a certain kind of success: they display great assiduity and skill in the silencing of dissident voices. Once again and as always, a supposedly liberating revolution ends up as an extremist tyranny.

I cherish this phenomenon of 'Progress and the Golden

Future' rather perversely, although in personal detachment from its theory and its practice too. It appeals to the part of me that relishes gaslight and Tennyson and the poems of John Betjeman: it is so splendidly dated, so essentially Victorian a hope! "Steam and the electric telegraph, my dear Sir, will. . . ."

If there is to be real hope for us, as Catholics or otherwise, it will not be of that sort.

What form could it possibly take?

Let us at least admit the difficulty of that question. A great many people, if not "the mass of men", do lead "lives of quiet desperation". It is not easy to see how they can do otherwise.

How desperately some people try to make out that the human problem is a simple one with an obvious answer!

> So many gods, so many creeds,
> So many paths that wind and wind,
> While just the art of being kind
> Is all the sad world needs.

Well, it isn't. Imagine that we have mastered that art perfectly and practice it unremittingly: we are still stuck with death and with many kinds of suffering if not with all. Only the suffering caused by unkindness has disappeared: we still face cancer, bereavement, taxes, and the dreadful passing of youth. Beyond all such things, we still face the absurdity of our own existence in a seemingly meaningless universe—the fact of our own guilt as well, unless we reduce *all* moral evil, unrealistically, to simple unkindness.

And in any case, we haven't mastered that art perfectly and don't know how to do so.

Ella Wheeler Wilcox is there being just about as helpful as you would be if you said to a starving beggar: "It's quite simple! Stop being poor, be rich instead!"

That would only heighten the beggar's despair.

What could ease our own despair?

One difficulty about that question is that many of us now belong (in effect) to a new species, hitherto unknown to history and anthropology. We differ from all earlier specimens of *Homo sapiens*, in that we have grown up without *any* particular notion of human nature and destiny, of where we come from and why, of where we are going and how, of what life is all about. Practically all our forebears, primitive and civilised, had answers of some kind to that range of questions—answers which we may think irrational and absurd but which were supportive none the less, giving the individual a frame of reference in which to conduct his life. But about that range of questions, most of us have been programmed since childhood into something more than a mere scepticism—a genuine nihilism of the mind. Every influential voice has told us that life has no particular meaning or purpose; that man is nothing but a specialised mammalian species of doubtful viability, accidentally thrown up by a blind evolutionary process; that there are no objective rights and wrongs anywhere; and that death is the absolute end of a story that adds up to nothing at all.

That doesn't go for all of us, of course. But it goes for a great many; and I suspect that it's this, rather than apocalyptic fears of that Bomb, that throws so many young people into a despair of which their characteristic musical addiction is one clear symptom.

A despair, and—very often, in that popular music—a

manifest diabolism. The hero of *Brighton Rock* believed in Hell more easily than in Heaven: if faith in the goodness of God has been held back from you, faith in the power of Satan is very likely to take its place.

Among the factors that make for existential despair nowadays, should we not include advertisements, in the press and on the small screen?

It is a primary function of advertisements to generate unreal needs, and then to generate illusions about how these may be satisfied. So they constantly hold before us varied images of a Perfect World.

We all know this Perfect World. The sun shines there permanently: one is forever about twenty-five and handsome, always with that average advertisement sort of face: one's wife is forever about eighteen and very pretty, and one's two children (boy and girl) are forever twelve and ten respectively. Everybody smiles all the time: even the man who delivers the milk or the mail is smiling. The car is always new and clean, the house is well maintained and in order and is a very nice house anyway, the garden blossoms profusely. Everything is permanently perfect; and all because you bought the right sort of detergent or cereal or laxative.

There are actually two sorts of despair which this vision can generate. The first stems from fear that we may never attain that Earthly Paradise: the second stems from fear that we may, in fact, attain something horribly close to it.

We would then go out of our minds with boredom.

Boredom is one prime mode in which we experience existential despair, and the two great remedies for it are the two supremely exciting things, sex and violence. Television addresses bored people for the most part, which is why it makes assiduous use of those two remedies.

How desperately people seek relief in either or both! The urge to sex—or to fantasy-sex, which many of us seem to prefer—is usually recognisable for what it is; but the urge to aggressiveness and violence conceals itself under a thousand disguises. The book reviewer may need to examine his conscience, the religious controversialist too, and anyone whose bosom swells with righteous indignation about some political cause. Such people may of course be right in what they say. But while it's one thing to have a burning zeal for truth, it's quite another thing to use truth as a pretext for aggression, physical or verbal.

There is much talk nowadays—rightly—about the moral question of modern war. To my mind, all such talk is quite unreal unless rooted in a constant awareness that men *love* war—also every kind of sub-war, challenge and confrontation and conflict in every possible version. When we hit and kill—literally or figuratively— we are satisfying one of our deepest lusts: we are also replacing boredom with a supreme kind of excitement.

Nowadays—sad to say?—the scientists have made actual war into a damnably expensive and dangerous business. But there are many substitutes for it, satisfying enough as escape-routes from boredom.

And of course sex costs nothing and doesn't kill anybody.

Its attractions are obvious enough, and they go far beyond the simple pleasures of the body. It extinguishes boredom, it enables us to forget all about death and suffering and guilt and alienation—for a time, that is. In varying degrees, the same is true of gorgeous food and drink, of riotous fun and jollity in every version. "Eat, drink, and be merry, for tomorrow we die."

Those familiar words add up to one possible and indeed popular response to the raw human condition. The trouble is that with that skeleton at the feast, authentic merriment will be easy to simulate but hard to achieve in anything like the long term.

In the short term, the demon drink has a lot to be said for it. There is a poem which tells how a wise old hermit had the whole problem of our condition put before him and replied in the simplest possible way: "Come, my lad, and drink some beer." Housman echoed him:

> Malt does more than Milton can
> To justify God's ways to man.

If we drink enough beer, the problem will certainly seem to go away. But it will return in the morning, compounded by a bad headache; and if we attempt to stay drunk *all* the time, we shall be courting early death.

That, in itself, could be one answer to the question. The act of suicide is performed by some and is—I suppose—considered by most of us at one time or another, in however distant and theoretical a manner. It has sometimes been regarded as an act of heroic courage and sometimes as the ultimate in cowardly escapism; and on the most favourable assessment, we have to share Hamlet's anxiety about whether it really does end the story, and with it, the despair of our condition. There are some who maintain that it can only make that despair more total, eternally inescapable as well.

But as Camus observed, this question is philosophically central. Our existential *Angst* can be stated in theoretical terms: "What are we here for? What's the point of being alive?"; and in practical terms, this becomes "Why bother to go on being alive?" A certain animal instinct usually makes us cling to life, blindly and tenaciously. But it is clear that like our other instincts, this one is capable of being disciplined and overcome. The question of whether and when we should overcome it is a central one indeed, and it must be faced by any religion or philosophy of life that hopes to be taken seriously.

In my present context, one point is of particular importance. My subject is the possibility of hope, and we can certainly dream of easing our natural despair and even—less plausibly—of eliminating it altogether. But suicide is the exact opposite of all such aspirations. If we kill ourselves, we concede the ultimate victory to despair.

Perhaps there's only one remedy for the raw human condition: we must turn to the consolations of religion.

But is 'religion' a consoling thing? What kind of hope does it offer us?

Let us ignore its cruder versions, attending only to the highest subtlety and refinement that religious thought has ever attained outside the Judaeo-Christian tradition.

Most of us were brought up in that tradition, or at least in its cultural and psychological backwash; and some of us assume too easily that its central concept of a benevolent Creator will be found elsewhere too, and some kind of consequent hope. But it is not so. Outside that Judaeo-Christian tradition, it is the practically universal instinct of religious man—at his highest—to see either illusion or else disaster in what we call 'creation', in the act or process that causes all these different things to exist separately, all these different people in particular. Where the emphasis is placed upon the illusory nature of all such differentiation and multiplicity, all such separation from the One, some version of Monism follows: where a degree of reality, but of *evil* reality, is there seen, we get some version of Dualism. Either way, something analogous to salvation will be proposed, and therefore a kind of hope.

But hope for *whom*? This kind of salvation will involve the abolition rather than any healing of our raw condition. We shall cease to suffer. But as a condition of doing so, we shall also cease to exist as individuals, in the body at least and perhaps altogether.

I cannot take that last distinction very seriously. Can we really envisage a wholly spiritual salvation, with no resurrection of the body? I am sure of one thing: I simply wouldn't be 'myself' without my body, elderly and hideous though it now is.

But we should never underestimate the power and plausibility of those religious views—as found among the Gnostics and the Manichees, for example, also among the Hindus and Buddhists—which take a centrally negative attitude towards 'creation' and our condition in this life. For one thing, they resolve or by-pass the entire problem of evil, which is otherwise so perplexing. That problem only arises because we try to reconcile the experienced facts of evil and suffering with the existence of a Creator who is infinite in both love and power.

Some see this reconciliation as clearly impossible. Their case could be stated in almost syllogistic terms. If God is a loving Father, as the Christians maintain, he will want to make his creatures perfectly happy: if he is omnipotent or almighty, as the Christians maintain, he will be able to get what he wants. But we observe that the creatures—notably ourselves—are far from being perfectly happy. It follows that God (assuming him to exist) must be defective in love and benevolence, or else in power—or, of course, in both. Various options remain in theory. But the mere fact of suffering and evil means that the Christian option is ruled out absolutely, by the simplest kind of logic.

I have adapted that statement of the case from C. S. Lewis: in one version or another it has come home to all of us, as when a bereaved mother might cry, "Could God have prevented my baby from dying? If he tried and failed, I'm on his side, but I don't see how he can then be 'God' at all! But if he could have saved my little darling and chose not to, then he's an evil God, and it would be wicked to worship him!"

A dilemma indeed! But it vanishes as soon as we stop trying to reconcile irreconcilable things—as soon as we separate the idea of creation from the idea of benevolence, the idea of 'being' from the idea of 'goodness'. That's the highly plausible option of most religion.

But what consolation, what hope will we then have? There is certainly comfort of a sort, social utility as well, in any ordered pattern of thought that seemingly imposes meaning upon the otherwise chaotic and absurd flux of experience; and it is clear enough that the faith of the Hindu or Buddhist can bear rich fruit in fortitude, asceticism, spirituality, and wisdom. But in all such versions, religion widens the scope of despair. We all know that great disasters happen within this life of ours. But we are now told that our entire present condition, our existence as separate individuals especially, is disastrous in itself and always must be. Escape from this, even into something indistinguishable from non-existence, constitutes our only real hope.

But that's no hope for 'you' or for 'me'. It's as with suicide: for us as individuals (and what else are we?) the ultimate victory is conceded to despair.

"But *we* know that God is love!"

Do we?

One should have patience with all men. But I find it very hard to be patient with the blind fatuity of those who say "God is love" as though it were a platitude. It's either a flat lie, or else it's a never-ending paradox, a mystery of faith. What it can't be is an obvious truth.

The loveliness of God's creation?

Blake gazed in awe upon his tiger: "Did he who made the lamb make thee?" But what about the insects that lay their eggs in the living bodies of other insects? Was it a God or a devil who thought up *that* one?

We sit here by the fireside, discussing theodicy or the problem of 'love almighty and ills unlimited': we are well fed and comfortable, we have port and cigars. Then, casually, we switch on the radio and listen to the late news. It tells of contention and carnage and disaster, so we switch it off again and resume our discussion. We are surfeited by horror nowadays, the media force a whole world's agony upon our attention, so deadening any possible response to it. And the despair and blood and death in tonight's news were remote: it was all happening among poor people in some remote corner of the globe.

So we drink some more port, and consider God's love

for his creation; and as you sip and ponder, you are suddenly distracted by a thought which you have been trying to put out of your mind for quite a time: shouldn't you go and see the doctor? That little swelling is entirely painless, but it does appear to be getting larger. . . .

So, perhaps, did one of your Neolithic forebears find himself stalked by a sabre-toothed tiger, and—so far—painlessly.

God is love?

Let us not speak lightly of the 'consolations of religion', let us not invoke the name of God *easily*. Pascal the Jansenist knew full well that in the absence of a Redeemer, the existence of God is *bad* news, not good news at all.

Suppose that you'd never heard of him: imagine that you have somehow gone through your entire life without ever meeting or entertaining the faintest notion of a Supreme Being and a further life. Now, utterly tired and spent on your deathbed, you look forward to the relief of total extinction. The story hasn't been altogether miserable, but it has been exhausting: thank God it's nearly over!

God? Suppose you now heard, for the first time, that you were not about to escape from existence at all, but only from time and change; that you faced an eternity as what you now were; that by way of transition to that eternity, you faced arraignment before a Judge of absolute justice from whom no secrets were hid, and least of all, the dirty little secrets of your past life; and that from the start, this same Judge had most urgently desired to be your friend but had been consistently ignored and rebuffed by yourself, not only in the more obviously dirty of those secret moments.

Would that information comfort your death-bed?

Time makes our sufferings endurable and our joys imperfect, since it tells us that both will end. But what if the escape from time and change offered us sufferings that were unendurable or joys that were perfect, since neither would end at all?

It could hardly offer us both.

But what falsity there is in all that I've said so far! Do I see life in terms of unrelieved gloom and despair, with suicide as the most obviously sensible response to it? No, I most certainly do not: do you? "There's night and day, brother, both sweet things; sun, moon, and stars, brother, all sweet things; there's likewise a wind on the heath. Life is very sweet, brother; who would wish to die?" Being optimistic by temperament and in many ways fortunate too, I warm more naturally to Borrow's words than to all those assertions of doom and gloom. The mystery of all being can certainly fill us with existential dread, but it can also fill us with simple delight and sometimes with a kind of serious awe, as André Malraux found: "I encountered many times those humble or exalted moments when the fundamental mystery of life appears to each of us as it appears to nearly all women looking at a child's face and nearly all men looking at the faces of the dead."

At such moments—they are not always our happiest moments—a most powerful intuition takes over, in defiance of all pessimism and its seeming logic. Even the most sceptical of us then feels aware of a close connection between the ideas of 'being' and 'goodness', so that any separation of them would be false to his own experience. "Something tells him that the ultimate idea of a world is not bad or even neutral", said Chesterton; "Staring at the sky or the grass or the truths of mathematics or even a new-laid egg, he has a vague feeling like the shadow of that saying of the great Christian philosopher, St. Thomas Aquinas, 'Every existence, as such, is good.' "

To such moments if not to the whole of life, one's proper and indeed natural response is gratitude. But to whom? It has often been remarked that the atheist's worst moment comes when he feels grateful but has no one to thank. You cannot really thank Evolution or the blind forces of Nature.

I would put the case more strongly. Imagine that you were recently at the point of bankruptcy but then received extraordinarily generous help from a wealthy friend or perhaps from some anonymous benefactor. Being suddenly elevated to wealth, you naturally want to thank him; and if he insists on remaining anonymous, you feel a painful sense of frustration. But even if you do know who he is, you still feel a sense of embarrassment, of insufficiency. It's easy enough to say "Thank you!", but it's so far from being adequate: what *can* you say? "Thanks a million times" is stilted, absurdly mathematical. Words fail you at such a moment: the sensation of "I simply don't know how to thank you enough!" can be a painful one.

That particular pain is not one that we need to take very seriously, and least of all in that financial version of the case: there are worse things in this world than the embarrassment of the suddenly rich. But in the wider scene, the immeasurable gift of existence generates a real problem. It is when the goodness of all being comes most sharply home to us—our own being especially— that mere 'religion' proves most crucially insufficient. If there is a God, it may perhaps enable us to forgive him for making such a dreadful world. But will it enable us to thank God suitably and sufficiently for making such a splendid world, and for putting us into it?

But all that was just an intuition, a mood or feeling of certain moments. Bleak reason takes over before long, telling us that there cannot be *honest* talk of thanking God until we have solved that unresolvable problem of evil. As for our condition in general, the ugly facts remain and appear to have the last word, now as in Neolithic times. Life, in this too-familiar human world, is far from being uniformly unpleasant. But it does seem altogether point-less, and this casts a shadow of despair over everything. Birth, life, and a fever of activity; sex and more birth; good moments, but bad moments of suffering and guilt and anxiety as well; the incurable sense of alienation and exile; the slow failure of body and mind and then good old death, the whole story adding up to nothing at all.

Then why are we here? What is life for? Does it have any meaning and purpose? Does it even make sense for us to ask whether life has any meaning and purpose?

Such questions aren't just teasers for philosophy: they are existentially present and troublesome, though often inarticulate, in all human experience. They might per-haps be represented as boiling down to a single question, one that is capable of at least two answers. It concerns the relationship between those two concepts 'being' and 'goodness', which are fundamental to all possible think-ing. How are they related? We are happy in our good moments and unhappy in our bad moments. But overall and in general, *is it a good thing for us to exist and be alive as human beings?*

"No", say some deeply thoughtful and religious

people; "Our existence in the body and in this world, although endurable, is essentially delusory or evil or both."

"Sometimes yes and sometimes no", say others of great influence nowadays; "It's a good thing to live when certain minimum satisfactions and comforts are more or less guaranteed. But where life entails severe and inescapable adversity, it's a positive evil."

Upon what basis, if any, could we find a third answer?

One thing is clear at least: if we do ask questions about the meaning and purpose of life—and we can hardly refrain from wondering—we shall be presupposing the existence of God, perhaps unconsciously. We shall not necessarily be presupposing the existence of a *benevolent* God: we may well be querying or denying his benevolence. But we shall be taking it for granted that some kind of personal God is there to have his benevolence queried or denied. Meaning and purpose only exist in the mind of a responsible agent: in the absence of such an agent, those two words make no possible sense.

I stare uncomprehendingly at a text printed in—say—the Hungarian language. A few of the words may suggest English words to me, mostly by accident: if a good many of them do so, I may be able to suppose that I have gathered the drift of the whole text. But if we ask for its real meaning, we won't find this in the ideas that it accidentally puts into my head on those lines: it's what was put into the text by the mind of its Hungarian writer.

Wrecked on a desert island and with just a few random articles washed up on the beach, you might find yourself in possession of a corkscrew but no wine. So placed, you might conceivably find some use for that corkscrew, as a tool or weapon: to the question "To what use can corkscrews be put?" you would then have a kind of answer. But in order to answer the different question "What is the purpose of a corkscrew?" you need to refer back, ultimately, to the mind of whoever made it.

So with this life of ours. To the question "What sense can we make of it, what can we do with it?" various different answers can be contrived. But if we ask "What *is* its meaning, what *is* its purpose?" we shall be referring back—however unconsciously—to the writer or manufacturer, the responsible agent: we shall in fact be asking "What is God up to? What on earth does he think he's doing?"

If there is no God, such questions are of course meaningless. But I have no great faith in the existence of atheists.

It would certainly annoy the scholars if the Greek word *logos* were to be translated as 'the meaning and purpose of life'. Yet there are New Testament usages in which such an understanding of it could perhaps be defended.

What *is* the meaning and purpose of life? I don't think it would be altogether fanciful to read the opening sequence of St. John's Gospel as an answer to that very question. "The meaning and purpose of life? Oh, that was there in the beginning: it was with God, and in fact it *was* God. . . . And the meaning and purpose of life became human and lived among us. . . ."

Semantic Interlude

'Being a Catholic': what does it *mean*?

It depends on what you mean by 'mean'. There is one sense in which it 'means' nothing—or nothing of any importance—except where the unchanging facts of our raw condition are borne steadily in mind. So long as our attention is taken up with preoccupations and problems that are particular and local and temporary in nature, it is bound to seem like an irrelevance.

That's how it seems nowadays to a great many people; and in this respect, there has been a conspicuous change during my own lifetime, a big shift of emphasis. When I was a young man—already addicted to this vice of religious controversy—I frequently met people who said in effect and in one version or another, "Your religion isn't true." Their present-day counterparts are much more likely to say, "Who cares whether it's true or not? Why should anyone bother about that sort of thing?"

How do we explain this shift of emphasis from truth to relevance? One obvious factor is a rise in general scepticism, a decline in intellectual curiosity, a mounting suspicion that there's no such thing as 'truth', and least of all in religious matters. It's all a question of how you feel!

Beyond that, affluence and technological development have made it much easier than it was to live in a state of insulation from primary experience, and also to be distracted by a constant barrage of verbal and visual stimuli. Our condition is thus made somewhat less raw and much less inescapably raw: we find it easier to pretend. Death is still there, of course. But we go some way towards pretending that it isn't. We treat it as an embarrassment, bundling it out of sight as completely as we can: unlike primitive people and the Victorians, we seldom go in for grand funeral panoply. Suffering is still there, of course. But we do our best to see it as an anomaly, a failure of the system, something that can and should be put right. Earlier generations knew that one needed the virtue of Fortitude in order to make life endurable: many of us appear to think that one shouldn't need that virtue at all and that anyone who finds things harsh and painful is suffering a grievous injustice and can rightly complain. So with personal guilt, also our sense of alienation and our "immortal longings": we do our best to explain these things away psychologically and to distract ourselves from their haunting presence by a thousand activities and stimulations.

That leaves us with the seeming pointlessness of our existence, the fact that life appears to have no meaning or purpose at all. Curiously and indeed perversely, many people cope with this ultimate despair by *celebrating* it, hoping thereby to draw its sting. The distinctively 'modern' movement in the arts can be seen as one vast exercise in that sense.

So, by evasion and pretence, people are enabled to forget their real condition; and in view of its inherent despair, we can understand their anxiety to do so. A Faith for which so many were once prepared to live and die (and even to kill) thus comes to seem like an irrelevance, a thing of no particular interest one way or the other. It is about our real condition: it never set out to be about our pretend-condition.

But it's only in a specialised sense that 'meaning' is a matter of relevance, of how we are caused to take an interest. In that sense, 'being a Catholic' gets its 'meaning' from the raw human condition. But there's also the question of what the word connotes, of what Catholicism *is*; and here, we come across a great deal of confusion, largely verbal or semantic in nature.

Some of this is of fairly recent origin. A powerful myth or hallucination has lately been going the rounds, to the effect that 'being a Catholic' now means something utterly unlike what it meant (say) thirty years ago. For the most part, this fantasy stems from wildly over-dramatised notions of what the Second Vatican Council was and did—as though it intended to usher in a kind of New Dispensation, one in which the liberal–Catholic intelligentsia would be on top and would call the shots, even in matters of faith and morals. Many such people, often of great influence, thus consider it honest to offer ideas and opinions and preferences that are strictly their own as though they were something more—as though they added up to some new and definitive notion of what 'being a Catholic' has now got to mean. No wonder that concept gets thrown into confusion and seems wholly vague and uncertain to many! There has in fact been a positive desire to empty it of all real meaning and importance for the sake of a crudely–conceived ecumenism: as many people see things, it mustn't be allowed to signify anything momentously different from (say) 'being an Anglican' or 'being a Methodist', to look no wider.

But earlier and more strictly semantic factors have also been at work. That word 'Catholic' and the two related words 'Christian' and 'Church' have long been subject to various kinds of stress and have so taken on ambiguities

that are not always noticed: each of the three has gathered
sub-senses and side-meanings to itself, and the net effect
is to make religious discourse needlessly difficult and
(too often) sterile.

I have offered my reflections on *not* being a Catholic,
on the raw human condition: now, by way of preparing
the ground for my reflections on *being* a Catholic, I shall
attempt a little semantic repair-work on all three words.

Let us consider 'Christian' first of all.

It is of course a religious word: as a noun, it refers
to one who is a baptised and believing disciple of Jesus
as 'the Christ', the Anointed One, the Messiah of Israel,
the Son of God and the world's Redeemer. The old
Evangelical formula is beyond criticism as far as it goes:
"When I call myself a Christian, I mean that I accept
Jesus as my personal Lord and Saviour." But a tricky
question then arises: "Do you do so on his own terms, or
on some other terms that are more congenial to yourself,
or to people you respect, or even to twentieth-century
thought in general?"—and that raises the further question
of what the Lord's terms are, and of how we find out
about them. The Evangelical is ready with his answer.
But to my mind, although sound in many particulars, it
is an answer that would only make real sense if the New
Testament had dropped straight down from Heaven,
neatly bound in black and with an attached note that
read, "This, and this alone, is my saving Word or
Message for humanity: (signed) GOD."

That didn't happen. The Church was there before
the Gospels were and long before the New Testament
existed as such. When the curtain rises in the earliest
Epistles, it shows us the Church already in action,

already a going concern, already possessed of that dogmatic and monopolistic confidence which incurred so much dislike in its later manifestations, and (it seems) with no primary interest in the formulation of a new Scripture. If a file of its earlier documents—many of them 'working documents', as we might say—came later to be called 'the Word of God', this was the outcome of an ecclesiastical and partly liturgical process, and rather a slow one at that: it happened by no directly divine intervention. Historically speaking, the New Testament—considered as a whole—is a fairly early and partially definitive publication of what it is now customary to call the Roman Catholic Church.

In that statement of the case, the reader will catch echoes of many ancient controversies, and he may be disposed to disagree. But my present purpose is semantic rather than controversial: my point is that whatever we say or deny so far, we shall not be throwing the meaning of 'Christian' into any great confusion. Its implications may be debatable: its broad sense is clear and unequivocal.

But this word has recently undergone a remarkable semantic transformation, and this does generate confusion. There are numerous contexts and usages in which it has practically ceased to be a descriptively religious word and has become an evaluatively ethical word instead. In much adjectival use, though not in all, it has become almost synonymous with 'unselfish' or 'altruistic' or 'socially benevolent'.

Something of that sort is now the word's dominant sense in most ordinary conversation. A good Christian, people feel, is an unselfish person: he thinks much of others, seldom of himself: he is slow to anger and quick to forgive: the ruling values, even the ruling passions of his life are care, concern, compassion, community, sharing, peace, and love.

That (people feel) is *true* Christianity, as seen in positive or sometimes in negative terms. "For pity's sake, can't you be more of a *Christian* about this?" The man who thus speaks in exasperation is not necessarily rebuking your failure to take the Incarnation into account, the Passion, the Resurrection: he may not believe in anything of that sort. He may well mean nothing more than "Do you *have* to be so selfish and bloody-minded about this?"

Even when thus given a purely ethical meaning, the word still echoes the name of Christ; and it is no rare thing to meet people—they are obviously not the ones most deeply soaked in Scripture—who suppose that "Love your neighbour as yourself" was an *original* recommendation and precept of Jesus, his own distinctive contribution to religious thought and practice, and hence the distinguishing mark and message of his followers.

Where that delusion prevails, it is sometimes possible to administer a salutary shock by asking whether a Jew, Moslem, Hindu, or atheist is capable of being 'a good Christian'. In that ethical sense he clearly is, and he often acts accordingly, sometimes putting us to shame. But if the question is raised in that form, even the least attentive and the most broad-minded will notice the incongruity of attaching that particular label to such people.

The truth is that there is nothing distinctively Christian about altruism, or dedicated social benevolence, or even "Love your neighbour as yourself." In various versions —"Treat others as you would wish to be treated", for example—this has always been central to all developed ethics or morality everywhere. Consequently admirable behaviour-patterns are not even peculiar to the human race. Much animal behaviour is unselfish or altruistic, in the sense of being socially but not individually advantageous. The worker-bee who stings you will usually die for Queen and Hive.

Let me not be understood as trying to cut unselfishness or altruism or social charity down to size, as of no real importance. But it does make for confusion when we talk as though 'Christianity' meant precisely that. For one thing, we then make the concept of 'Christian unity' even more elusive than it would otherwise be.

Let us now turn to the word 'Church', ignoring the sense in which—when given a small *c*—it means 'a building used for Christian worship'.

In its primary sense, it refers to the *ekklesia* or assembly of the baptised believers, the Chosen People of the New Dispensation, seen not simply as a human society but also as a continuing mode of the Incarnation, the one-and-only Body of the one-and-only Christ, speaking with his voice and operating by his presence and power. Thus Paul, persecuting the Church, could be accused of persecuting Christ himself.

As so seen, the Church is inherently one: the word cannot go into the plural without changing its sense. The New Testament speaks of the different 'Churches' of this place and that place, but in a sense that is slightly but clearly modified. Every such 'Church' was something more than a part of the one *ekklesia* and something less than a separate and independent thing: it was a local presence or incarnation of that wider unity, self-sufficient in certain senses but not in others, living only by the

common faith and life of Christ as mediated through the
Apostles, the universal episcopate everywhere. There
could still be certain differences and discords within the
Church, human nature being what it is. But beyond
a certain point, any serious break or rupture would
be unsymmetrical in nature. It would not leave us with
two 'Churches' in any full sense of the word, or even
with a single but now divided Church. It would involve
a unilateral departure from the unity of Christ. That
would remain what it always had been: alongside it,
there would now be a heretical or schismatic body—a
sect or denomination, we might prefer to say in this age
of euphemism.

Every such departure was seen from the start as a
moral evil and a serious one, as was any subsequent
maintenance of the consequent *apartheid*. Various factors
could palliate the guilt of individuals: this could disappear
altogether, formally speaking, especially in later generations. Materially speaking, however, any sort of *apartheid*
between Christians would always be something flatly
opposed to the Lord's emphatically declared wish and, as
such, a wickedness or sin.

Later developments have altered the picture radically,
as we see from the fact that the word 'Church' can now
go into the plural as freely as it chooses. There are a great
many different Churches: as currently envisaged, they
exist side by side and more or less on equal terms, their
separation being very unlike the merely geographical
separation of 'the Churches' that we find in the New
Testament. In most usage, the word now suggests a
voluntary association of 'Christians' (however that word
is understood) who happen to share a common outlook and a common tradition and who come together
accordingly. On this reckoning, while one's 'Christianity'

(again with that qualification) is a thing of great, if vague, importance, one's membership in some particular 'Church' is very secondary. It may be decided by inheritance and custom and preference, or nationally, or politically, or socially. In England, a distinct social gulf used to separate the respectable people in the Anglican Church from the lower classes in their Nonconformist chapels. I have heard of a railway town where—in the good old days of steam—your place of worship was determined by your place in the railway hierarchy. When you rose to the high dignity of being an engine-driver or engineer, you could properly call yourself 'Church of England'—a title that would be mere social uppishness if claimed by some lowly porter or fireman. In just the same way, an American who attained higher social dignity would sometimes mark the fact by joining the Episcopal or Anglican Church.

In recent years, the existence of denominational *apartheid* has come to be recognised more and more widely as a regrettable thing, even as a shocking and most deplorable thing. Should 'Christianity' come in all these different versions? Should 'Churches' (in the full plural) exist at all? But in my experience, their separate existence is usually seen as an undesirable state of ecclesiastical politics, such as we can hope to see remedied by negotiations and a little give-and-take on either side, also by mutual involvement at the grass-roots level. It is seldom seen as a matter of personal morality: where it is, an extremely powerful prejudice or taboo decrees that any guilt must be shared equally and by all parties, as must any repentance and repair. The consequence is that while aspiring to 'Christian unity', we effectively prevent ourselves from doing anything about it, and even from thinking about it with any realism. In many circles, the key six-letter words 'heresy' and 'schism' (which refer to two versions of Christian disunity) have become as unutterable as those four-letter words were until recently.

But the internal contradictions of ecumenism, when seen as a road to unity, lie beyond my present purpose. The semantic point is a clear one. The word 'Church' is currently used in a number of very different senses.

In the first place, we use it in one sense when we speak of the Church of England or the Methodist Church, but in quite another sense when we speak of the Universal or Catholic Church. In the former cases, the word means 'sect' or 'denomination': we imply that any number of such Churches can exist, regrettably (no doubt) but altogether lawfully as things now stand. In the latter case, however, we refer to something which cannot possibly exist in the plural—something, moreover, to which every follower of Jesus has a duty of full adherence. This distinction will give offence to some people. It is a real one, none the less, essential for any full understanding of what 'being a Catholic' means. Where it is overlooked, people naturally come to see the Universal Church as a sect or denomination that has got ideas above its station.

Some further distinctions of usage remain, even with reference to that Universal or Catholic Church alone. Some writers draw one of them nicely by saying 'she' when they want to emphasise the unblemished Bride of Christ and 'it' when they want to emphasise the imperfect human institution: in much the same way, Maritain distinguished the *personne* of the Church from its *personnel*, while not suggesting that these were two wholly separate and unrelated things. Beyond that, we can use the word more widely or more narrowly. In many contexts, 'the Catholic Church' refers to the entire *ekklesia*, the community of all those who profess the complete Faith and are in the full Unity. But there are other contexts in which it refers to the Apostolic Hierarchy alone, the Pope and the Bishops.

This latter usage bothers some hypersensitive people: they take it as suggesting that the following of Jesus is an essentially clerical affair, with the laity added on as a kind of unimportant appendix or afterthought. It was never so understood in my experience, and there is no real reason why it should be. When we apply the name of a whole to a specifically functioning part, we use a common and perfectly legitimate figure of speech. "The United States has recognised the new regime in Banana-land": that makes perfect sense, even though there are over two hundred million Americans, only a few of whom took any active part in that decision. No such usage implies that the great mass of Americans are people of small account, constituting a mere appendage to the State Department.

It is interesting to note that a parallel usage—'the Church' meaning 'the clergy'—was once very common among Anglicans but practically unknown among Catholics. "My son is going into the Church": that was a perfectly normal way of saying that he was going to be a parson. The Catholic equivalent for that was "My son is going to be a priest" or even "My son has a vocation"— and there, once again, we gave a usefully specialised sense to a term of wider import. We thus reminded ourselves that the priesthood was a matter of obeying God's call, not just a job or career: nobody ever supposed that this was true of the priesthood and the religious life *alone*, no matter what those current hypersensitivities may imagine.

Theologically speaking, various understandings of the word 'Church' are capable of being defended. The important thing is to be conscious of the word's complexity and clear about one's intended meaning: otherwise, confusion and cross-purposes are going to prevail.

The word 'Catholic' raises problems of its own, even where used in its dominant sense of 'Roman Catholic'.

It does have various secondary senses. We can of course ignore the non-religious sense in which a man might be said to have 'catholic' tastes in music or poetry. But it has two more specialised religious uses. As found in the Creeds, it is commonly understood by Protestants as referring to an invisible Great Church—the Platonic *idea* of all Christianity, of which these sects and denominations are partial and imperfect copies. It is also used in Anglican circles to indicate something or somebody of the Anglo-Catholic sort, as distinct from the more Evangelical element within the Church of England. (That Church did something which I deplore: it created an atmosphere in which the words 'Catholic' and 'Evangelical' could seem antithetical instead of complementary.)

In most contexts, the prefix 'Roman' can be omitted without serious risk of confusion. Imagine some Anglo-Catholic being approached in the street by a stranger who asks, "Excuse me, can you direct me to the nearest Catholic church?" Even today—certainly in the recent past—it might be his instinct to reply, "Do you mean a Catholic church of the English or of the Roman obedience?" But if he did, he would be making a point. He would be in no real doubt as to what the enquirer was looking for, even if no rich brogue were audible.

Even so, the word carries hidden ambiguities which can easily generate confusion, and do in fact generate vast confusion nowadays.

How can this be? Isn't the Roman Catholic religion an extremely clear-cut and sharply-defined thing? People have often complained that it's far *too* clear-cut, far *too* much a matter of precise definition at every point. But however deplorable that may be, doesn't it at least confer the semantic blessing of clarity? 'Being a (Roman) Catholic': isn't this among the most precise of all such concepts? We all know perfectly well which of our friends and neighbours are Catholics and which others are not; and as for the Catholic Faith itself, while it includes 'mysteries' in a technical sense, it is not otherwise 'mysterious'. It is amply on public record: you can read it up in any number of books.

And yet there is semantic confusion, and of two kinds.

In the first place, while the word suggests some general identification with the well-documented Faith of the Roman Catholic Church, the degree of identification that is implied can vary enormously.

At one extreme, it is used freely and confidently where the implied identification has little or no religious content. The word then becomes nothing more than a badge of tribal or family or even political identity. Among certain ethnic groups in the United States, for example, Polish or Bavarian or Italian as the case may be, the words "I am a Catholic, of course" may occasionally mean only "I identify strongly with my Catholic forebears and kinsfolk, I am not prepared to make a public break with our own people." The speaker may be quite candidly an agnostic or atheist, though he may retain a desire— strictly 'superstitious' in nature—to be buried with

Catholic rites when the time comes. In traditionally
Catholic parts of Europe, a similar declaration will
sometimes mean only "I hate the Communists"—or the
Socialists, or the Masons, or all three. (The converse can
sometimes be true in such places. "I am a Communist"
may imply no faith at all in dialectical materialism and
the dictatorship of the proletariat: it sometimes means no
more than "I hate the fat priests.")

These are extreme cases. Anyone who says "I am a
Catholic" will usually be making a religious statement
about himself.

It will seldom be a statement about his notable sanctity
or even about his tolerably virtuous conduct: unlike
'Christian' in so much present use, 'Catholic' has never
been a strongly ethical or moral word. When so invoked,
it will normally be a kind of religious self-description,
mostly in terms of institutional membership, very much
as this might be explained by the canonist. A Catholic is
then—as it were—a card-carrying member of a visible
organisation, though he carries no actual card.

So far, so good. It is when we move on from membership to belief—to faith and morals—that we find major
ambiguity, and world-wide confusion in consequence.
In that connection, it is possible and indeed commonplace
to find two men, and even two priests, each of whom
describes himself as a believing Catholic, but in a sense
radically different from that intended by the other. The
two are in flat contradiction. Whatever might be said
theologically, it is semantically most unhelpful that the
same word should be applied to both.

To indicate the nature of their contradiction, I will
have to speak crudely of something very subtle. 'Being a
Catholic' is, among other things, a matter of belief: it

involves some kind of assent and agreement with what I shall crudely call 'the tradition and teaching of the Church'. But that assent or agreement can be of two radically different sorts, leading to very different conclusions and also to fierce arguments.

It's rather like the difference between learning from a competent teacher and agreeing—more or less completely —with a group of fellow-students, the subject being one in which none of you has any independent *expertise*. One can always have opinions; and in the latter case, you would be pleased to find your own opinions shared, broadly at least, by this group. It might then be your instinct to associate with its members, to identify with them, on the basis of their general agreement with yourself. But this identification would always be conditional. At any moment, as you pursued this subject in the absence of a competent teacher, you might decide that your fellows were grievously mistaken about some particular point. You might then try to convert them to a better way of thinking: alternatively or as well, you might loosen your ties with the group.

At no stage would there be anything wrong in these developments—not unless you all succumbed to a common failing of enclosed groups and began to see your shared opinions as universal certainties. But you would all be in an entirely different situation if a highly competent teacher came among you, qualified and certificated in every possible way, knowing the truth of the matter where you students can only have opinions.

Much of what the teacher tells you may well sound baffling and even absurd. That's because you've still got a great deal to learn; and of course you can ask as many and as searching questions as you like. Some of these will be answered at once. But you may sometimes be told that only very advanced students can hope to understand the answers. The main point is that, while you are entitled to contradict your fellow-students, you are not entitled to contradict this teacher. There is no possible basis upon which you can do so.

That's roughly analogous to the two different meanings which 'being a Catholic' can have in matters of faith and morals. One man says, "I'm a Catholic: that is to say, I go along with the teaching and tradition of the Church because it corresponds pretty closely with my own preferred manner of thinking, and in so far as it does—I naturally dissent where it doesn't." But another says, "I'm a Catholic: that is to say, I accept the Church as teaching in Christ's name and by his authority. There are grey areas and unresolved questions. But where the Church's voice clashes unmistakably with my own preferred manner of thinking, I have to accept correction. There, I was in the wrong. There's no intellectual basis on which I could claim to know better."

There are intermediate cases: the 'I know better' syndrome—it's usually a matter of 'We know better'— can be a mild and localised infection and not the terminal paralysis which it frequently becomes. But broadly speaking, we can say that 'being a Catholic' has now acquired two radically different meanings so far as belief is concerned. One man gives the 'assent of faith' to the teaching and tradition of the Church: the other only gives it the selective assent of his critical judgment. This may sound like a quibble, but its implications and consequences are momentous.

The reader will not suppose that I am theologically neutral in this matter. But I am here trying to be semantic more than anything else, concerned only with words and their handling, with the eliminating of ambiguity and confusion. My point is that this word 'Catholic' is often uttered in one of those two senses and understood in the other. The consequent cross-purposes will benefit nobody.

But I would like to make one further point, logical in nature. Any man is at full liberty to give the selective assent of his critical judgment to the teaching and tradition of the Catholic Church. I don't quite see how he can do this in an intellectually responsible way, since the subject-matter lies beyond all human experience and verification in this life. But let him try.

What is easily overlooked is the logical *emptiness* of any claim which he then makes to be a believing Catholic. He will be saying in effect: "I agree with the teaching and tradition of the Church, except where I disagree with it." This will be true but logically void: it will in fact be a tautology. Anybody can say that about anything. I myself agree with the Moslems except where I disagree with them: I do not call myself a Moslem on that account, and would consider it highly misleading to do so. I also agree with the Marxists, the Baha'is, and the Duck River Baptists except where I disagree with them. But to say this is to say nothing at all.

As a matter of some urgency, I think we need to devise some clear and agreed-upon terminology, value-free and offending nobody, by which the two opposed senses of 'a believing Catholic' might be distinguished in common usage. Some such terms are in current use already, but they are far from being value-free and are often short on accuracy. Can we not devise some inoffensive word with the general sense of 'fellow-traveller', to indicate those who wish to be identified with the Catholic Church in some broad fashion which might include technical membership, while only buying its faith and morals on their own selective basis?

There would be ample occasion for using such a word.

The word 'Catholic'—in its sense of 'Roman Catholic' —is also subject to a further and quite different kind of semantic malfunctioning. This makes for a different kind of confusion.

Over the last four centuries, historical factors have caused this word's reference to become curiously narrowed, and in two related ways. In the first place, it has come to suggest, chiefly or even only, those things which needed assertion because the Protestant Reformation had denied them—Church as against *sola Scriptura*, visible unity as against fragmentation, *magisterium* as against 'private judgment', discipline as against dissent, and so forth. Neither in its etymology nor in its early history does the word exclude these things. But it does carry certain wider implications, and these have sometimes tended to be overlooked. We might almost say that it then becomes a negative term: 'being a Catholic' has long suggested a pattern of thoughts and words and deeds which said at every point "The Protestants are wrong!"

A man might believe that the Protestants *were* wrong, from the start and seriously, while not wishing to put so central an emphasis upon the fact for today's purposes. That (he might feel) is not the primary message which present-day people need to hear from the more reliable messengers of Jesus.

In the second place and relatedly, the expression 'Roman Catholic' has come to suggest not only *a* Church—one of many—but also a cultural particularity which, being of limited relevance, tends to obscure its meaning. I sometimes find myself wishing, therefore, that common usage spoke of the Universal and Petrine Church instead. 'Roman Catholic' calls up a number of images that are hardly 'catholic' at all, being one-sidedly flavoured by the Mediterranean region and the Counter-Reformation period: it makes some people think vaguely of immensely tall candles in exuberantly decorated churches, of certain flamboyant styles in prelatical finery, of the swooning or gesticulating saints of baroque statuary. In the city of Rome itself, one might gather a foolish impression that the real object of Catholic worship was the Italian Renaissance.

You don't have to eat garlic in order to be a Catholic: whatever the ghost of Belloc may assert *de fide*, you don't even have to drink rough red wine with every meal.

Now I enjoy both garlic and wine, I won't hear a word said against the Italian Renaissance, and I don't share the impatient Puritanism of those who find only embarrassment in the whole Catholic inheritance of the Counter-Reformation period. I value that inheritance, its liturgical and devotional and cultural styles included: beyond that, I would say that certain associated styles in clerical behaviour were far more defensible than many people are now willing to concede.

Semantically speaking, however, it remains true that 'Roman Catholic' now carries side-meanings and over-tones that would be absent from 'Universal and Petrine' and are (for many purposes) irrelevant and distracting. It seldom suggests what it ought to suggest—a particularly intense and integral understanding of 'Christian'.

I suspect that those accidental associations of 'Roman Catholic' go a long way towards explaining the embarrassment which that expression, or even 'Catholic' alone, can generate in some. "Yes, yes, I was brought up as a Roman Catholic, and in fact I still do live within that tradition; but I'd much prefer to be considered simply as a Christian." In certain cases, such words would indicate hyper-ecumenism or some other weakness in specifically Catholic belief. But I have reason to suppose that in others, they are prompted by nothing worse than semantic discomfort.

The words 'Christian' and 'Catholic' have thus drifted into a distinctly uneasy relationship. They can even come to seem flatly antithetical, as in the Irish use of the former word to mean, specifically, 'Protestant'. My wife and I once took one of the babies along to be baptised, and, when the priest turned up, I said, "Come on, let's make this little heathen into a Christian." A pious Irish lady heard me and was deeply shocked. "Ah, no—you should make him into a Catholic!"

But the uneasiness is there, even in less extreme usages and understandings, conveying various kinds of false impression. 'Christian' comes to seem like an ethically evaluative word, as I have observed, and 'Catholic' like an institutionally descriptive word alone. The one suggests love and the free Spirit, the other suggests rules and a harsh discipline: the one is for gentle selfless people, the other is for assertive bullying people. I have heard it said that while 'being a Christian' will make you into something of a Leftist, 'being a Catholic' must inevitably propel you some way towards the Right. I also remember a priest who said, "My parishioners are excellent Catholics—I wish I could see some hope of making them into Christians!" Logically speaking, this was an absurd thing to say. As most of us see things, every Catholic is *a fortiori* a Christian—perhaps as every Virginian is *a fortiori* an American or perhaps otherwise, but somehow at least. And yet we know exactly what that priest meant. Perhaps unjustly, he was saying that his parishioners were good at law but bad at love, good at letter but bad at Spirit: they were in fact a bunch of Pharisees.

If that's what 'being a Catholic' means, we had better be something else.

But that's nothing like what it means, of course, in its etymology and its earlier history and in good modern usage. That priest was using the word in a specialised and rather perverse sense, to indicate a particular corruption to which some Catholics—and many others—can sometimes and in certain circumstances be prone. His quip was an instance of how side-meanings can cling to a word like barnacles to a ship.

Scrape the word clean, and you come up with something like the following.

'A Catholic' is simply a Christian *tout court*, one who follows the Lord *kath holou*, according to the completeness or entirety of what that following is, with no *hairesis* or selectivity. It was baptism that made him into a Catholic in the first instance: this incorporated him into Christ and therefore into the Church—into *the* Church, the one-and-only body of the one-and-only Lord. (That's what it does to anybody who is baptised at all, whoever does the baptising and in whatever sort of building. It's a kind of category-mistake to speak, as some people do, of being 'baptised into the Church of England'.)

Beyond that, when we call a man 'a Catholic', we are saying something negative about him. His incorporation into Christ's Body has not suffered damage in two particular ways: since his baptism, he has not got into a bad relationship with the mind of the Church (he is not a heretic) or with its body (he is not a schismatic, he has incurred no ecclesiastical penalty). His Christianity remains its integral self, a complete and organic incorporation into the Lord.

What, under grace, has he made of it? That's quite another question. He is not necessarily a saint: he may be the worst of sinners, and unless his sins have been such as to incur excommunication, he will be no less of a Catholic on that account. We describe him as a Christian *kath holou* or completely, but we then refer to the completeness of what he is supposed to be attempting, the completeness of the equipment at his disposal, not to the height of his actual achievement. That will be whatever it is: sometimes poor, sometimes splendid, never sufficient, seldom to be judged by others.

All this amounts to a suggestion that when the two words 'Christian' and 'Catholic' are in semantically good shape, they are normatively synonymous.

I often use them accordingly, in the general interest of clarity and good usage. In all matters, if we seek clarity, we naturally speak of completeness as the normative thing. When a human being is mentioned, it is naturally assumed on both sides that he or she has two eyes and can see reasonably well, even though we know that there are some blind people. Among our fellowmen, tolerably good eyesight can be taken for granted in the absence of specific mention to the contrary: it is the normative norm and—fortunately for us—the statistical norm as well. (The difference is important. Imagine some frightful epidemic that leaves nine-tenths of the population permanently blinded. Vision will now be statistically exceptional. But nobody will call it an 'abnormality' on that account.)

Ideally—though seldom, in practice, without explanation—one should handle the word 'Christian' on the same lines. In the absence of special mention to the contrary, it should be used and understood *kath holou*, with reference to the whole of what the following of Christ normatively entails: it should naturally be taken to indicate completeness rather than selectivity in the Faith, and also full unity with the See of Peter and so with the whole Body. In most contexts, the terms 'Catholic' and 'Roman Catholic' would then be redundant, as otiose as the expression 'two-eyed' would be if applied to most of your neighbours.

It's the abnormalities and malfunctions that call for special mention—though seldom for rebuke, and never for contempt.

I once suggested—to a Cardinal at Rome, no less— that the Church ought to set up a Sacred Congregation for Vocabulary and Semantics. A great many of its practical difficulties lie in that area. There is, for example, a problem already mentioned—the problem created by those theologians and other writers who are Catholic by institutional membership but not by belief, and who therefore confuse millions. I do not propose harsh penalties for them: only accurate labelling.

So it is with an individual writer who sets out to reflect upon his own experience of 'being a Catholic'. He needs to explain his own use of the relevant key words. Present-day usage makes for cross-purposes: it gives continual unnoticed reinforcement to such ideas as that 'Christianity' is essentially a matter of social altruism; that 'a Church' is a voluntary association of like-minded Christians; and that 'Catholic' stands to 'Christian' as a particular species stands to the wider genus. Many people —possibly including some readers of this book—find it extremely difficult to think outside the consequent mind-set: communication then becomes impossible without preliminary explanation.

That's how I justify an interlude which might otherwise seem out of place in such a book as this.

Chapter Two

Our Homeland's Embassy

"I am a Catholic": that is certainly a true statement.

"I am a good Catholic": that is certainly not a true statement. But then, there aren't any good Catholics. We are all failures, "unprofitable servants", and a great saint is one who recognises his personal failure most acutely.

But I am still a Catholic. What does that statement mean, when considered experientially and existentially rather than in semantic or canonical or even doctrinal terms?

Where I grew up, Catholics were very much of a minority, tolerated at last after centuries of persecution, but somewhat isolated from the mainstream of English life, and not only because a large proportion of them were immigrants from Ireland. To people of other faiths and of none, the Catholics seemed to be a distinctly idiosyncratic minority, a 'peculiar people': they had odd ideas and odd ways, and these aroused mild interest and mild curiosity. Few people bothered to find out how their minds worked, and why.

Twice a week, their odd practices might make some limited social impact upon others. There was, firstly, their observance of Sunday. Others might sleep late on that day of rest, or perhaps go to church if they felt like it. But these Catholics had a service called 'Mass', to which they attached tremendous importance, despite the fact that it was conducted in a language which few people understood: they *had* to go to Mass on Sundays and on certain other days. If you had Catholic guests, you needed to take this seemingly obsessive necessity into account. It could mean early rising or a late lunch, travel-arrangements perhaps, some general dislocation of the household.

In common speech and the common understanding, this curious compulsion was the definitive element in 'being a Catholic'. This *meant* 'going to Sunday Mass': neglect of the practice would entail an effective loss of the title. In some circles, it was thus possible to say "He calls himself a Catholic, but he doesn't *go*"—the "but" being strongly disjunctive. The same assumption prevailed in the United States. Once upon a time, in Connecticut, I was the guest of a middle-aged couple, the husband being Irish by name and ancestry. Over the wine, he found occasion to say that he was a Catholic and always had been. "You a Catholic?" cried his wife in affectionate derision; "You call yourself a Catholic when, to my certain knowledge, you haven't set foot inside a church for twenty years!"

There was another thing you needed to remember, on another day of the week, if you had Catholic guests. For some unfathomable reason, these people were obliged to eat fish on Fridays. In vain did they plead that this was a negative discipline of not eating meat: in the popular mind it remained, unshakeably, a positive injunction to eat fish. In fact, this Friday abstinence was even more compulsive than Sunday Mass. There were some people who ignored the latter duty for years on end, like that man in Connecticut, while still feeling constrained to abstain punctiliously. To do otherwise would be to repudiate one's identity. Many Catholics have confessed that when that discipline was changed in more recent years, the first Friday hamburger felt like an apostasy and led to a kind of identity-crisis.

For many, therefore, 'being a Catholic' was not so much a matter of what you believed or how fervently you prayed or how virtuously and altruistically you lived. It was primarily a matter of what you did on Sunday morning and of what you ate on Friday.

Further things were of course known about the Catholics. They had a superstitious veneration for the distant figure of the Pope: they insisted on having their own schools, sending their children to no others, as though in fear of pollution: as soon as this subject became mentionable, they stood out as people who were supposed not to use contraceptives.

Others looked more closely and spoke more sharply. Catholicism (they said) was an insidiously powerful superstition, a devil's corruption of true Gospel Christianity. For one thing, Catholics were idolaters. They worshipped statues and a piece of bread, a wafer or cracker: you could watch them doing it. Then, they worshipped—at the best—a Mother-Goddess rather than God the Father. Their favourite devotion was known to be the Rosary; and there, for every utterance of the Lord's Prayer, there were ten appeals to the Blessed Virgin. And they were forcibly held down in their bigotry and superstition, forbidden to read the Bible and all other religious works not certified by their blinkered authorities, for fear that they might commit the sin of thinking for themselves. As for the Pope—well, if Rome were not actually the Scarlet Woman, the Whore of Babylon, it was something pretty close. At the very least it was a tyranny, a dictatorship: Catholicism was to religion what Fascism was to politics. Weren't nearly all of them automatically on Franco's side? Didn't nearly all of them automatically oppose every idea and movement and tendency of the modern, progressive, liberal sort?

One particular criticism was offered consistently and often, even by some who were otherwise kindly disposed. Catholics were people whose Christianity had fossilised into a rigid institutionalism; they attached a wildly exaggerated importance to their particular Church as against all others, and they saw practically all religion —faith, morals, worship, everything—in terms of punc-tilious obedience to its authoritarian structures. This gave them a narrow and un-Christian crabbedness of mind. If only somebody would throw open the windows of the Vatican and let in a little fresh air! That was most unlikely to happen, of course. But unless and until it did happen, a thoughtful Christian had to see Catholicism as a kind of relapse from the New Testament back into the Old, a Pharisaism, a cult of letter as against Spirit and of law as against love—a precise instance, in fact, of the kind of thing from which Jesus had tried to set us free.

That's how it looked from the outside, to many at least, and even to some who saw it from the inside; and it is hardly to be denied that such an impression had some basis in some of the facts. But was that an overall realism? How centrally was 'being a Catholic' an experience of that kind?

If you shifted your angle slightly, remembering the raw human condition and rising above certain quasi-political tensions in the mind, you could get a very different picture.

The writer Helen Waddell was, like C. S. Lewis, an Ulster Protestant. In *The Wandering Scholars* and elsewhere she offered well-researched but splendidly romantic evocations of the Middle Ages and also of what some still call the 'Dark' Ages, despite the illumination and creativity that one finds in that period upon closer inspection.

She was an intensely perceptive writer. "I'll never be a Catholic", she said, "but I'd never get my work done if I didn't now and then dive into that strange divine sea."

The *rightness* of that haunting phrase!

The sea has many voices, speaking contrapuntally in Eliot's poem *The Dry Salvages*: it shows one face to children on a summer beach, another to the scientist, another to sailormen in rough weather. In one mood it will reflect the heavens most peacefully, in another it will be all storm and fury. I'm more than a little scared of it, even at the best of times. In *The Rime of the Ancient Mariner*, it becomes nightmarish.

'Being a Catholic': the strangeness, the divine and (above all) *oceanic* quality of that condition can easily get forgotten, what with the fume and fret of our daily preoccupations, as can the raw condition which it replaces and remedies. But then, unexpectedly, it hits you once again.

It escapes some people altogether. What they see is more like a municipal swimming pool, roofed in and heavily chlorinated and strictly regulated, with instructions and warning-notices posted up on every wall and rigidly enforced by uniformed male attendants. One could of course learn to swim in such a pool. But the experience would be very unlike that provided by "the rude imperious surge".

That's a limitation of vision: such people miss the point.

The experience of 'being a Catholic' always included restrictive and abrasive elements, as must any steadily-maintained contact with reality. So far as this life is concerned, it's only in fantasy that we can have all things free and easy and exactly to our liking. In this respect 'being a Catholic' is very much like being married, right down to the irksome obligations, the monotony. It's also rather like the experience of being found guilty and sent to jail, and—just about equally—like the experience of being found innocent and set free. It's a curious mix of the easy and the difficult, not to say the impossible. God is easy to please but hard to satisfy: Heaven is free but not cheap.

Some have described the Catholic Church as the natural or proper home of mankind. But what a double-edged word 'home' is! It refers to where we come from, where we belong, but it always includes possibilities of "If I don't get out of here, and *soon*, I'm going to SCREAM!" (None the less, home is where you creep back, broken and bleeding, to die.)

But if it's a familiar place to be, it's also a strange place to go. This life is a journey, not a destination: half our troubles stem from foolish attempts to treat it as a destination, or to find some destination within it. Given this preliminary fact, 'being a Catholic' means that you aren't lost. You know where you're going, and how to get there. (But of course you don't *know* your destination in any real sense of imaginative or even intellectual apprehension; nor can you do your own navigation, or provide your own motive power. If anybody had ever been able to do those two things, the raw human condition wouldn't be so tragic and filled with despair.)

In retrospect, I believe that this distinction between 'journey' and 'destination' will—in certain senses— disappear. But we are stuck with it for now, and with various warnings that the journey was never likely to be an altogether comfortable one.

What a strange vehicle we travel in! We can't always see how it works, or why: it can present one set of appearances when seen from the inside, and another and totally different set when seen from the outside. Its outward appearances are by no means always of that harshly institutional and authoritarian kind. There are undoubtedly some who see Catholics as people who live under an unnecessarily rigid discipline of thought and behaviour. But, quite as often, one finds them *envied* in a curiously romantic way, as a privileged people who are mysteriously in the know, their Church being some- thing esoteric, an in-thing, an international Freemasonry or Secret Society from which others are excluded and so made to feel vaguely inferior.

I have sometimes heard wistful complaints in that sense. "But others *aren't* excluded!" I protest; "The doors are wide open, anyone can come in!"

"Yes, that's just what makes it so maddening."

In the autumn, English schoolboys play competitive games with conkers, so called because those games were originally played with *conchae* or snail shells.

Not all varieties of the chestnut tree produce conkers

as their nuts or fruit, but *Aesculus hippocastanum* does,
and I have a splendid specimen in my own garden. Every
autumn or fall, I am briefly a conker-millionaire and a
generous one, to the great benefit of the local schoolboys.

But for me, this tree does something else as well: it
provides a perfect metaphor for the Church.

Consider each of its fruit as found, especially in the
earlier days of the conker-season. On the outside, each
looks distinctly unattractive: it has a thick, stained,
shabby, hard, leathery skin, covered with small sharp
defensive spikes. But when you break this skin open and
look within, you get a very different picture. You find
the nut or conker itself, and it's a thing of unutterably
perfect beauty, brown in exactly the rich and variegated
way of an old violin, with a touch as of milk on one side;
and it lies in what can only be called a bed of white satin.
The harshness of that skin was on the outside only, and
for purposes of cherishing and protecting.

So with the Church: harsh and spiky on the outside,
"all glorious within".

A cliché of our time: "Religion? Yes, of course, I'm
entirely in favour; and I think I can call myself a 'Christian' in the deepest sense of the word. . . . But I haven't
any time for *institutional* religion."

Rather a self-righteous sort of cliché, but understandable enough, especially at a time when we are
all drowning in regulations, paperwork, bureaucracy,
and government nonsense of every kind. Hence the
adversative overtones of that word. It makes us think
immediately of grey men in offices, manipulating us all
with their lists and files and figures. Can 'religion' be a
thing of their institutional sort and still be of value? Can

'the Body of Christ' have telephones and filing-cabinets and still remain itself? How can such things conceivably have relevance to the bloodstained Cross and the flames of Pentecost?

Many people have long objected to Catholicism on such lines. Some of them will have sustained a recent disappointment. In the 1960s and 1970s, the ice appeared to be melting: the Church seemed to be becoming much less rigidly institutional, much more human and open. But now, at least so far as 'Rome' is concerned, it shows distinct signs of reverting to the old pattern. People sigh heavily: for one thing, there were various ecumenical hopes that once seemed plausible and now seem less so.

When this subject comes up for discussion and complaint, I always feel like pointing out how extraordinarily *little* institutionalism there is—by present-day standards —in the day-to-day life of ordinary Catholics. Elsewhere, life is a web of papers and cards, of lists and licences: look at the regulations and documents and the checking-up that will be involved when you make an international journey, for example, or set about the purchase of a house, or simply try to live your own life without getting into trouble with the government! In your life as a Catholic, there's practically nothing comparable. Nobody checks up on you. Approach the altar at some place where you aren't known: you will not be asked to produce your Certificate of Catholic Identity, your recently-stamped Absolution Form. Analogous things are demanded everywhere else, but not there: you are numbered and card-indexed and computerised in just about every other aspect of your life, but not in your Catholicism. People sometimes complained that the old Code of Canon Law hardly mentioned the laity, as though they were diminished thereby. But the case was otherwise. Within the Church, law and administration hardly existed at all except in respect of the small professional minority, the clergy and religious. The rest of us were practically free of all such things, unencumbered by institution and paperwork, trusted and taken at our face value at practically every point, with marriage—which is subject to some regulation in every possible society—as the primary exception.

The terrible Roman Curia? Yes, if you like. Four hundred years ago, Papal Rome did look rather like a Renaissance princedom, and now it has come to look rather like a modern bureaucracy: we find a comparable development locally, in every diocese and even in every parish. But when the worst has been said about this bureaucracy, it remains minute in scale. Compare the total number of ecclesiastical bureaucrats to the total number of Catholics: then, in your own country or world-wide, compare the total number of public officials to the overall population. Will you then have the nerve to say that by present-day standards, the Catholic Church is too institutional, too bureaucratic?

"But should it have that character *at all*, even in the smallest degree? Shouldn't it be concerned solely with love and the Spirit?"

I distrust all such sentiments profoundly: they suggest Gnostic or Docetist leanings, a feeling that only the disembodied or 'spiritual' can be good and that the real Church has to be invisible, as for some Protestants. In the last analysis, they suggest a distrust of Incarnation.

"But all these arguments add up to one big cop-out. All right, your Church hasn't got so very many bureaucrats or so very much paperwork. But it's the most tremendously institutional thing none the less, like a strict and even totalitarian government: it gives orders, it lays down the law, it does its best—even now—to silence dissent, it instructs and regulates most crabbedly, it imposes strict discipline at every point. Some of your theologians talk about 'the priesthood of all believers', but it doesn't add up to a row of beans in practice—the actual ordained priests still carry on as though the Church were a tightly-disciplined army, with themselves as the officers and with the Pope as Commander-in-Chief. That's the kind of thing we don't like: that's what seems so alien to the spirit of Jesus."

One small comfort for such a critic: that officer-corps is in distinctly ragged shape nowadays.

But where such things are said, I always feel not that the critic has got his facts wrong, but that he has completely missed the point. His appeal to the "spirit of Jesus" is of course sentimental and selective. Beyond that, however, he has failed to take into account the nature of the situation that we're in and of any possible remedy. That's why, writing about 'being a Catholic', I saw fit to begin with some heavily insistent gloom about 'the raw human condition'. We overlook that by habit because it's so painful: we then miss the point of the proposed remedy.

As a way of bringing that point into sharper focus, reasoned argument will not always be very effective. Meaning rather than truth will be the thing at stake, and I shall do what I can with a scatter of images or metaphors.

Not that the practical difficulty is always of that kind. I have met countless people who rejected the Catholic Faith and even poured scorn upon it, not in some subtle missing of the point, but in straightforward ignorance, such as could be remedied by half-an-hour in any good library. Time and time again, I have heard a scornful "You Catholics actually believe that . . .", and have replied "But we don't, and we never did!"

It's all too human to indulge strong hostile feelings about something not understood. Defoe said that there were a hundred thousand country fellows in his time ready to fight to the death against Popery, without knowing whether Popery was a man or a horse.

'Popery'—insufficiently so called, though the Pope does play one key role within it—is neither a man nor a horse; nor, contrary to popular belief, was it ever some kind of hang-up on institution and rigidity. It is, above all, a matter of love and hope; and if we fail to see this, it's because we are looking at it from the wrong angle and with irrelevant preoccupations in mind, having forgotten what the raw human condition is.

'Loving the Church': that is undoubtedly one big part of what 'being a Catholic' means. But how easily that former phrase can be misunderstood! How plausibly but how mistakenly it can be taken as referring always to a distraction, even an idolatry! And yet, it is only the old twofold Commandment made into one. In loving the brotherhood we love Christ's Body, we love Christ, we love God: in loving God, we also love the brotherhood, his presence and operation and voice within the historical process, his Embassy upon this planet.

To some, of course, that expression 'loving the Church' might suggest something apparently different and much less holy—a kind of romantic ecclesiasticism, perhaps. But where this exists, how different and how much less holy must it be?

Let us consider an extreme version of it. If one moves in literary and academic circles, one occasionally comes across a man who cultivates romantic ecclesiasticism for its own sake: he makes the externals of Catholic history and life and practice into a hobby, a richly colourful aestheticism. In my experience, he commonly turns out to be excellent company. How keenly and wittily and with what a wealth of erudition he holds forth about—say—the history of the Mozarabic Rite, or the politics of Arianism, or the intricate protocol by which the honorific use of the thurible is governed! For such a one, the difference between 'canons regular' and 'clerks regular' is the most obvious thing in the world, and when it comes to plainsong, he has strong opinions for or against Solesmes: he is on dining and gossiping terms with any number of monks and Monsignori, and he may well be able to tell you the scandalous inside story of some latest ruction within the Roman Curia. He shakes his head most sadly, of course, over recent ecclesiastical re-adjustments: their overall tendency has been to reduce the scope and interest and colour of his hobby's subject-matter. But one can always ignore them.

Such a man will undoubtedly 'love the Church', but in a sense wholly compatible with agnosticism or even atheism on his own part. For that reason and otherwise, many of us—on detecting something similar in a fellow-Catholic—will rush to swift and severe judgment. Any 'love of the Church' which takes that form, any romantic ecclesiasticism, is out of place in a disciple, a true Christian. It will be an irrelevance at the best: at the worst it will be a Pharisaism, a concentration upon externals, even an idolatry.

I have sometimes met Catholics who, being hypersensitive to such dangers, spoke almost as though one needed to *hate* 'the Church' as so conceived. But I am made uneasy by such people, as by all severe Puritanisms: I get a feeling that the point is being altogether missed. Have they never been in love? Have they never noticed how love operates in action?

When a young man is deeply and romantically in love, he idealises his sweetheart on lines which the rest of us—not being so afflicted—may find slightly absurd, if engagingly so. She is the most beautiful girl in the world, he tells us; there is none like her for kindness of heart, sweetness of nature, for intelligence, for wit. Then we meet her; and while we find her a very pleasant young lady, nice-looking as well, we see nothing so very exceptional about her. Her attractions and merits are real enough but could easily be paralleled elsewhere. Truly is love said to be blind and a madness!

But our cynicism, however gently and kindly meant, is inappropriate. The young man is right. For reasons that are glandular in the last analysis, he has started to see one human being as God always sees all human beings—in the unique individuality of each, and with total love.

There are several things to notice about his love for her. For one thing, it is uncritical: by Cupid's mysterious alchemy, even her faults and limitations—or what you and I take to be such—are transformed into ingredients of her total charm. This will make for trouble, later on, if they get married. But now, it's simply one part of love.

Then, we don't rebuke him for concentrating upon externals. He speaks in awe of her beauty, and shows us her photograph by way of proof: it's an ordinary photograph and not an X-ray; it shows her skin rather than her bones and entrails, and it features the extraneous beauties of garments and jewellery and hair-style as well as her own beauty. It is no less a photograph of 'her' on that account.

Then, the young man's behaviour illustrates the fact that while love focusses upon its object, it also focusses —with no deflection or loss—upon things associated with that object. For this young lover, there's magic in the mere name of his girl: it's his *mantra*, he murmurs it to himself incessantly, though he knows perfectly well that there are other girls so named. When parted from her, he sees a train which is going to her home-town, to *her*: it becomes a magic train at once. When he thinks that there's nobody looking, he takes out that photograph of her and kisses it fervently.

An observer might conclude that his love for her is qualified: she has to share his affections with some superstitious cult of name-magic, with railway transport, and with photography. If he really loved the girl, his attention would be wholly upon her.

But such an observer could never have been in love.

Another angle, another picture:

Let us suppose that you are an American citizen and love your country, but you are compelled by the exigencies of your career to reside in Moscow.

You manage to live there contentedly enough, and in many respects as a Muscovite: there are roubles and kopecks in your pocket, not quarters and dimes and nickels. You feel no hatred at all for the Russian people but you intensely dislike the system under which they are compelled to live. Above all, you are aware of being an exile. There is a place where you belong, and this isn't it. You long to get back home, as in due course you will.

What, in the meantime, will be your feelings about the American Embassy here in Moscow?

It is an ordinary building, of course, and in most senses it is a Russian building. Within it, the American Ambassador presides; and I intend no disrespect for any holder of that office when I say that he will only be a man. He will not be a demigod; he will not be a mystical incarnation of Uncle Sam. He will in fact have his imperfections and—possibly—his serious professional faults; and if you have a lot to do with him, or if you simply listen to the gossip, you will become aware of these. You may even find it your duty, at one time or another, to make recommendations and efforts towards the better conduct of that Embassy.

But your normal feelings about it will not be of any such negative sort. In a real sense, you will 'love' it. When you enter it from time to time, you will be acutely aware of standing—just for the moment—on technically American soil. Everything there will carry the savour of home: there will be hamburger instead of caviare, bourbon instead of that eternal vodka, and the voices around you will entrance you by the mere fact of being American voices, whether they say interesting and important things or not. It will be with a definite reluctance that you eventually leave, going out into the alien streets of Moscow once again; and then, whenever the course of your daily routine causes you to pass the Embassy without going inside, you gaze upon it with a certain hunger, a certain love.

"This man claims to be a patriotic American, but he's

nothing of the sort: for some pathological reason, he's all hung up on one particular building in Moscow. Why, for Heaven's sake? Aren't there other buildings, there and elsewhere, that deserve his attention just as much?"

Would that be a sensible comment upon your habitual feelings, there in that place of exile?

When observed from the outside, love always appears somewhat obsessional, preoccupied with secondary matters.

A further angle, a further picture:

Let us consider parents who plan to take the family on holiday and—for the very first time—abroad. The children look forward to this in wild excitement: they can hardly wait. Now, a couple of days before departure, their father comes home from the travel-agency and shows them the tickets that he has just bought.

Consider those tickets for a moment. They are dull documents of the financial, legal, and administrative sort, with figures and details and warnings: regulations and conditions have been drawn up by lawyers and are here set forth in small print, with ominous mention of possible penalties and cancellations. All this reeks of business and the office-world: nobody could possibly love tickets.

And yet, for these dear excited children, the tickets are transfigured, bathed in a golden light: they are gazed upon with reverence and ecstasy. The children see right through the dull legalism—real and necessary though it is—perceiving only the Magic Carpet, the Key to the Door, the instrument that will make possible their wondrous journey over the sunlit sea and into the Peacock Lands.

Let's hope that they enjoy themselves when the time comes. No earthly holiday is quite as golden in fact as it was in anticipation. But one can enjoy it splendidly enough, especially in childhood, though often in ways that turn out very unlike what one had expected.

You and I are still children, explicitly warned by Jesus that we must retain or regain that character if we hope to find the one holiday-place that won't ever let us down. And just as a child of the right sort—a happy child, not yet made bitter by too much ugly experience undergone too quickly—will see glory in even the most pedestrian and commercial details of his approaching holiday, so also a Catholic *who really believes* will instinctively romanticise the Church, finding glory in even the most human and imperfect paraphernalia of its life—even in the priest who asks for money as that travel-agent did, even (if it comes to that) in the telephones and filing-cabinets of the parish house or the Vatican. (I know that there are telephones and filing-cabinets in the Vatican, since I've seen some of them; and I wouldn't put it past those people to have computers by now. But if so, you should see them as *special* computers, with at least a sparkle of the golden radiance. If you see them in any more pedestrian light, as dreary old computers and no more, it's because you've lost too much of your childhood, or because you've forgotten where we're going, or both.)

This does not mean that everything ecclesiastical is 'sacred' in the sense of being beyond all criticism: far from it. For my part, I want travel-documents to be well printed and conveniently set forth; and it's even more important that the regulations which get printed in small type ("Not valid unless . . .", "Passengers are warned . . .",

"Extra charges will be incurred if . . .", "In an emergency, OBEY THE CREW!") should be as easy-going and as fair and generous to the traveller as is possible in an imperfect world. We don't want people to be bullied and robbed by the airlines and the shipping companies; and if on the eve of their holiday we can persuade those excited children to come down from the golden clouds and attend to such questions, they will agree.

But their minds will be set on the glory to come, on what the dull tickets are going to do for them tomorrow, and they will only attend to those humdrum questions with a certain reluctance. Their inner eyes are already on distant horizons: "We would be at Jerusalem."

(And yes, you've guessed correctly: when thus writing of the dull tickets and the excited children and the happy holiday, I draw upon memory, not upon imagination.)

"The trouble with you Catholics is that you will enthrone legalism instead of love. Look at the incredibly complex rubrics that governed the Mass until recently! Everything had to be done *exactly so*, with every last gesture prescribed and regulated: there was no room at all for spontaneousness, for human authenticity! That's all been eased somewhat in recent years, of course. But my guess is that it will soon fossilise itself up again into that same old organisation-fetichist rigour: you people will never be really at home with the idea of freedom, you must have things laid down."

There could be something in such accusations; and yet, I am haunted by the fact that an appearance of pedantic legalism can often be given where the reality is nothing more sinister than appreciative love.

Within my household, at Christmas and Easter, we

have certain time-honoured rituals of family or domestic observance; and when grandchildren come, they are loud in their insistence that everything must be done 'properly'—that is, exactly as it was done last time. They look around with searching eyes, and if some decoration is in a slightly different place, they object. The precise observance of time-honoured rubrics is among the things that generate a sense of occasion, happiness therefore.

You find another version of the same instinct when, reading some familiar and beloved fairy-tale to a child, you rashly presume to alter it in some detail. The Wicked Witch had a black gown last time: now she has a grey one, and this might be deemed a bold originality on your part. But your youthful hearer will correct you at once: you have been guilty of a solecism, a failure in correctness.

This instinct for continuity and exact repetition appears naturally in the mind of a happy child: it is not some compulsion of the obsessed and fearful, and we should not be too hasty with such a diagnosis when adult love of some great happening finds similar expression.

"But when I grew up, I put away the things of a child." Not all of them, we hope: if you lost that protectively appreciative love for the great occasion, sacred or profane, and that consequent conservatism of rubric, you are the poorer for your loss. And the Lord never said, "Unless you grow up into disillusioned and restless adults, you shall not enter into the Kingdom."

A young man's love for his girl, an exile's longing for home, a child's eagerness for a golden holiday or for the rightness of a great occasion—in each of these cases, love wears an easy face, as it does in the corresponding aspects of 'being a Catholic'.

But elsewhere, love can wear a most exacting face, while not ceasing to be love on that account. Consider the operating-theatre during the long slow ritual of a heart transplant: consider the control tower at some airport, when a big jet with three hundred people on board and with two engines stopped is making its approach through a blizzard.

Freedom? Authentic self-expression? Doing your own thing? The glorious liberty of the sons of God?

Yes; but there's a time and a place for everything. The time for all that is when we're more or less on holiday. But can we ever take a holiday from the raw human condition on this side of the grave?

Have we forgotten what that condition is?

"The trouble with your Church", said a friend of mine, "is that it will *bully* people. I'm perfectly willing to listen to the ideas and recommendations of any man or institution. But I like to take my time and think things over: I don't like being ordered about and hustled along. Everything of that sort is such terribly bad manners; and that's always been the Catholic style. It puts people off."

I agreed, rather uncomfortably: I saw what he meant.

I had a curious dream that night. I saw a man sitting alone in his room, which was at the top of a high building, and writing a letter. By the magic of dreams, I was able to see into his mind: I knew that he was a philosopher and was writing to a colleague, one with whom he had long debated certain ultimate questions. Theirs was the most enjoyable sort of debate: that is to say, it looked like going on forever, saddling neither party with the burden of any final conclusion. So he was writing most happily.

Suddenly, in my dream, an amazing thing happened: the window shattered inwards with a loud crash, to reveal a grimy and helmeted face. The philosopher looked up in outrage. But before he could begin to protest, he was rudely shouted down.

"Come here! Quick! I can get you safely down this ladder if you do exactly what I say!"

"What on earth are you talking about? And what the hell do you mean by. . . ?"

"No time to argue, you fool, the building's on fire! It'll collapse in a few moments! Can't you smell the smoke? *Hurry!*"

Now this philosopher—as I knew by the magic of my dream—was a true lover of wisdom, well accustomed to the precise analysis of concepts. It was very much to his credit, I thought, that he overcame his natural anger at this intrusion and started to point out the weakness of the fireman's intellectual position.

"My dear fellow, don't shout at me like that. Yes, there is a smell of burning, now that you mention it; and it is compatible with the hypothesis that this building is indeed on fire, though of course with any number of other hypotheses too—strictly speaking, an infinite number. Now we should submit that question to empirical verification: if you follow Popper, you will agree that in principle, your assertion is capable of being falsified. But even if we assume—*dato non concesso*—that you're right on the question of fact, the question of value still remains; and I assure you that the experience of being carried down a very tall ladder, by a perfect stranger and in the dead of night, is one that can be assessed with equal validity in a number of different perspectives, not only in yours! And you gave yourself away, of course, when you demanded instant blind obedience to yourself as a condition of being saved. We've seen that kind of thing so often before—some fierce dogmatism, offered as 'the truth' when in fact it only expresses the speaker's desire to dominate and control. So, my dear fellow, if our discussion is to be a fruitful one. . . ."

But unfortunately, the building collapsed at that moment. The fireman had a narrow escape but survived on his ladder: the philosopher plunged down into the fiery depths, still philosophising as he went. How sad! He was a very good philosopher.

Then I awoke, and behold! it was not a dream.

Nobody can hope to understand the characteristic behaviour of the Church, or the point of 'being a Catholic', unless he habitually sees the human condition in terms of desperate urgency.

It is customary to speak of the Christian 'Gospel', the *evangelium*, the Good News. But any sort of good news can come in two versions, according to the continuing urgency of the matter in hand. There are some situations in which we can say, "It's all right! You can relax, there's nothing to worry about." But there are other situations in which we need to speak in different terms and—so to speak—in a different tone of voice: "Careful, now! You're in a hell of a mess, but I can get you out of it if you do exactly what I say!"

As a small boy, I was once silly enough to get myself stuck half-way up a dangerous cliff. It was in that second voice that my gallant rescuer spoke: it's the tone of my imaginary fireman and also of any real fireman in such a case. It's also the tone of voice in which Jesus spoke habitually and in which his Church has spoken ever since: it sounds urgent and commanding, perhaps even fierce, but it's still a voice of good news and of love.

As we know, it's also the tone of every bully, of everyone who is dogmatic and domineering by temperament. Even a good fireman, in his personal capacity, might be of that type. But that wouldn't make it very sensible for the philosopher to ignore or dispute his brusque commands.

The background questions are real enough. "Can this fireman really save me, on lines wholly determined by himself and calling for uncritical obedience on my side? Does he offer the only possible escape? Might there not be other rescuers, or even some escape-route by which I can save my own life?"

Such questions would need full treatment if this were a work of apologetics. But I am not trying to prove the answers, only to indicate the nature of the question. The house *is* on fire, our condition is one of desperate urgency. I have already considered the ancient reasons for regarding it as a condition of despair when honestly faced; and as for its urgency, we need only remember the fact that no man can guarantee himself a tomorrow. Your house—your life, your entire universe—will collapse under you sooner or later, at absolutely any moment and perhaps with no warning. You are now reading this book: what makes you so sure that you'll live to finish it?

That philosopher never finished writing his letter.

In order to cast some imaginative light upon those background questions, let us leave that fiery building and go back to the Second World War—to the year 1942, let us say.

An R.A.F. pilot leaves his aerodrome in embattled England and flies off on a mission to Occupied France. While there, he has a difference of opinion with a passing Messerschmidt and is obliged to descend by parachute, his engine being on fire. He lands safely in remote country and hides his parachute. What does he do next?

He finds himself in summer countryside of the friendliest, seemingly most peaceful kind. In a way it *is* peaceful: France is not an enemy country, though it is occupied by the enemy. An old peasant cycles by with bread and onions, paying no attention whatever to our pilot. But all such appearances are deceptive. The war is still going on: he must contact the Resistance Movement, the French Underground, and so get himself smuggled out and back to England. That's where he can best continue the fight.

But he needs to be very careful. What he must contact is the *authentic* Resistance, controlled and supplied from England, and he could easily make a fatal mistake. He starts to move on cautiously, and soon he meets some infinitely agreeable Frenchman and is offered help. But he can take no such offer at its face value. This Frenchman may be friendly indeed, as anti-Nazi as one could wish: he may on the other hand be working and spying for the Gestapo, as some Frenchmen did. And in any case, this pilot wasn't told to contact *any* group of helpful people: he was told to contact a very specific group, making sure that they were the right people. Until he has eliminated all doubt, by the careful use of some very arbitrary codes and passwords as briefed, a certain justifiable paranoia will be appropriate. His real condition is like the imaginary condition of the paranoiac: he is surrounded by unseen enemies, there are not many people he can trust.

The whole story is not of this sort. He knows perfectly well that there are some free-lance resistance groups, here in France, which would give him some kind of help and would never betray him: he also knows that some English pilots—when in his present position—have struggled through to the coast on their own account, with no French help at all, and have then stolen fishing boats and made their own laborious way home. But he is under clear orders to attempt nothing of that sort; and if he does, he will make things unnecessarily difficult and dangerous for himself.

Eventually he manages to contact the genuine Resistance; and his subsequent story, here in France, casts further analogical light upon some of the less alluring aspects of 'being a Catholic'. While being passed from hand to hand down to the Pyrenees—or wherever it may be—he will be among men and women who are working under great strain. They may strike him as being tough, hard-bitten, preoccupied people, hardly the company he would have chosen for easy relaxation, for the pleasant discussion of this and that. And they will speak in tones of harsh absolute authority: they will give him orders which seem utterly arbitrary to him, and which may well take him further from England in the first instance, not closer to it. He may be disposed to grumble and ask questions; he may want to have everything explained to him. But, if he does, it will be because he has forgotten what kind of situation he is in, what kind of struggle is going on.

He shouldn't have forgotten: from the start, it was

made clear to him that in this situation—or in the war generally—unquestioning obedience was going to be necessary, however uncongenial it naturally is to everyone's pride and self-will.

Slowly and in the teeth of great dangers and difficulties, and given his active obedience and effort, the Resistance will eventually smuggle him back home. It will never be a very easy journey; he will never be in full command of his own destiny. At some point, he may perhaps come across an opportunity to drop out and lie low—there in Occupied France—until the end of the war.

He has every good reason for resisting such temptations. He is still a man under orders; and while the war will end some day, it will not just fade away into nothing particular. D-Day will come, perhaps sooner than he expects: his King is going to invade in force, and decisively. And since he is a just King, it will then go very badly indeed with those who are found in some state of active collaboration with the enemy. But it will go quite badly enough for those who made no serious effort to find and identify the true Resistance, and worse still for those who merely decided to drop out of the arduous fight and take it easy.

'Being a Catholic' is very much like joining that authentic Resistance Movement. It will get you back to your Homeland. But you must not expect to enjoy every stage of the journey, or to like the people you have to obey, or to see the point of every order that they give you. Things aren't like that in wartime.

I have two reasons for liking that particular metaphor. For one thing, it makes England—however implausibly —into Heaven. Then, it corresponds to something in my own experience. I was never shot down into Occupied France. But in my distant R.A.F. days, I was carefully briefed about what I was to do in that event; and it struck me at the time that my situation then would be closely analogous to what 'being a Catholic' means, to the *kind* of its point and urgency.

But it's a bad metaphor in two ways. In the first place, while it's a disaster for any pilot to be shot down, it's no kind of disaster for a human being to get himself born into this world, enemy-occupied though it is, with Satan (according to Jesus) as its prince. The world itself is on our side; birth is a good thing. Then, while it was that pilot's sole business to get back to England as soon as possible, it is not the Christian's *sole* duty to get to Heaven in the shortest possible time. A long tradition authorises him to speak as though it were, as though longevity would be a curse: *cupio dissolvi et esse cum Christo*. But there's work for him to do first, here in Occupied France and partly for the sake of that country.

That metaphor might therefore suggest a Manichaean rather than a Christian and Catholic view of the human condition. So perhaps we should vary it with a different wartime picture—that of a secret agent, let us say, who is parachuted into France quite deliberately for an extended period. Such an agent also must contact the Resistance, with extreme caution and with some justifiable paranoia: he also looks forward to a return home and his Sovereign's approval. But in the meantime, here in France and in the face of the enemy, he has been given a job to do—some specific job of which he may fail to see the point, but for which he is uniquely qualified. When the war is over, he will see why that specific job needed to be done, and how it fitted into the Grand Strategy, and why he—of all people—was chosen to do it. But he can't expect to understand such things just yet.

Armies and intelligence agencies often operate on the principle of 'minimum information': you are only told what is strictly necessary for your immediate task. God appears to operate on that same principle, and Newman raised no objection:

> . . . I do not ask to see
> The distant scene: one step enough for me.

"You Catholics think you know all the answers!" they say. But we don't, and we never did. We only claim to have been told *some* answers and given *some* instructions, as from elsewhere, and with no implication that we're particularly clever people. God reveals himself in Christ, but very cautiously, only to the extent made necessary by the specific jam that we're in, the raw human condition. If he revealed *himself*, in any full sense and while we still remained in this life, we'd shrivel and disappear like a moth in a blast furnace.

Some of the saints and mystics have apparently come fairly close to such an experience. I suppose I ought to envy them, but I don't: I'm far too warmly attached to comfort and self.

But I do find myself in something not unlike an armed service in wartime, liable to the serviceman's kind of grumble. "The trouble about being a Catholic is that you simply can't call your soul your own": that's just what we used to say about being in the R.A.F. (But was your soul ever your own?)

Could there be something inept, even something slightly obscene, in the choice of these bloodstained metaphors for my present purpose? Aren't we talking about the Prince of Peace, his service and following?

They are bad metaphors in some ways, good in others. I tend to like Service people, considered as human types. But the older I get, the less friendly I feel towards wars and armies as such, and the more convinced that whatever one's problem may be, the violent answer to it is nearly always going to be the wrong answer. (I am constantly baffled by those people who, being intensely aware that the violent answer to the pregnancy-problem is the wrong one, none the less see a satanically violent answer to the Communism-problem as the right one.)

From very early days, however, wars and armies were seen as providing good metaphors for the Christian life. A *paganus* was originally a countryman as against a townsman, and, as early as the time of Tacitus, the word had come to indicate a civilian as against a soldier and was perhaps used contemptuously: townsmen have always despised countrymen and soldiers have always despised civilians, seldom with sufficient cause. (In those callow R.A.F. days of mine, we made both points at once by referring to the wretched civilians as 'farmers' or 'swede-bashers'.) Hence, in Tertullian, a *paganus* means someone who has not yet enlisted in the army of Christ. That gives the word 'pagan' its present sense.

So with my wartime metaphors, which are militaristic by analogy alone. A soldier or an R.A.F. pilot is (among other things) a trained killer, and if you dislike seeing the Christian compared to him for that reason, you have my sympathy. But if you dislike that comparison because it suggests orders and discipline—a state of affairs in which you cannot "call your soul your own"—then don't have anything to do with Catholicism or with Christ. Drop out of the war. Hitler will applaud you most warmly.

Even so, such metaphors can usefully be supplemented by others, less directly militaristic. There's the active, but there's the passive too: there's fighting, but there's also the experience of being liberated.

Let us suppose that we have always lived in a prison camp in some alien land. Conditions there are not too bad, and many of us contrive to have a good deal of fun. But it's still experienced as a prison camp and exile: most of us are haunted by dim, distant visions—ancestral memories?—of our Homeland and freedom.

Among us, there is much talk of liberation, naturally from the outside: it has long been clear that we cannot free ourselves. So deeply nostalgic are some people for home, so impatient for liberation, that they talk—often in great detail—as though the great day were almost or already upon us. Their minds are constantly on the pattern which liberation will probably or certainly take: they talk as though it were a present reality, and this gives them a great sense of comfort and relief.

But there are hard-boiled folk among us who rebuke all such escapist fantasising. There never was any Homeland, they say, or any hope of liberation. There's nothing for us to be liberated into: this prison camp is all that there is, and any delusions to the contrary are to be explained psychologically.

This strikes us as an uncomfortably plausible view of the matter. After all, we've never seen this supposed Homeland: all that we know of it comes by rumour and reportage and guess, together with certain intimate feelings that suggest a genuine folk-memory but could easily be deceptive. Wouldn't it be wisest to forget all that and—as those hard-boiled characters recommend— concentrate all our attention upon improving conditions here in the prison camp? We might then transform it in a way that would constitute the only true liberation.

Yet we cannot get away from all those persistent and pervading ideas about our own true country, the place where we would really feel at home. We have this incurable sense of exile: we may even feel it most acutely when prison camp conditions happen to be at their best. And we cannot help taking an interest in what those people say who fantasise—if that's what they're doing —about what the great day will be like. One group of such people claim to do so with particular authority, since (as they claim) they have received messages from our common Homeland. But we are not very much impressed. They seem rather grim and crabbed people, and they often talk as though our distant King were to be feared rather than loved. Would we *enjoy* liberation on his terms?

Let us now suppose that there is unmistakably solid news of an actual liberating invasion from that Homeland. The King has come! We haven't seen anything yet: so far, only a remote corner of this huge camp is free. But our turn will come soon: the great dream is actually coming true!

The hard-boiled sceptics are now clearly wrong, though of course some of them still say that they'll only believe it when they see it.

When it reaches us, it will and will not be a surprise. Its pattern will have much in common with the fantasy-versions of it which so many of us cherished before the event, as is natural enough: those were not random fantasies; they were rooted in long experience of what we were and what this prison camp was, and of how we experienced it as in exile and never as a home. There had also been some good thinking about what the Homeland of such creatures as ourselves would need to be like.

In some ways, therefore, liberation will be like what we had always expected. But in other ways, it will be utterly unlike anything we could possibly have expected, and even unlike anything we had supposed ourselves to desire.

Not all of us will take to it easily. As many people discovered after World War II, liberation—even from a prison camp—can be a traumatic and disorienting experience.

That's one metaphor for the Christian liberation, in its relationship to the things that foreshadowed it—the mythological dreamings of pagan religion and the astonishingly different foresight that was given to the Jews, and also (of course) the perennial scepticism of the materialist.

All religion can be described in terms of man's search for God: only this Christian and Catholic thing can be described in terms of God coming to the rescue of man. Christ stands in relation to the raw human condition as answer stands to question, as key to lock, as food to hunger, but most of all (perhaps) as liberation to jail.

It is of course a corporate or collective liberation. The Body of Christ is what crashed through the death-barrier and came out, transformed, on the other side: it's only by transformation into that Body, and therefore into one another, that we can do the same.

Into one another? Yes, and most crucially—even though this side of things has received some rather one-sided emphasis lately. Our liberation is no simple matter of 'community' in the sense of social altruism and togetherness: the Church does not exist primarily in order to remedy social fragmentation and the consequent loneliness, or—for Heaven's sake—in order to remedy social injustice by revolutionary means. But there is a two-way relationship between our love of Christ and our love of the brotherhood, the *ekklesia*: each includes and entails the other and, in the end, any distinction between the two comes close to vanishing.

We must naturally do our best to live in charity with *all* men. But that isn't what gets the scriptural emphasis: the thing stressed there is love 'within the family', as it were.

This can be difficult. There isn't always anything very much that's obviously and outstandingly Christ-like in one's Catholic neighbours: they seldom add up visibly to anything very strange and divine and oceanic. 'The Church' can in fact be something of a let-down, a disillusionment to the convert: there is such a huge, almost comical discrepancy between the vast claim implied in that expression 'the Body of Christ' and the human realities immediately perceived. All those stories about corrupt and wicked Popes are hardly to the point, though some of them are true enough: what gives the effect of a let-down is the *ordinariness* of Catholics, and perhaps of the clergy in particular. If there were anything in their massive claim, wouldn't there be something obviously remarkable about them?

For my part, I see that ordinariness as a kind of optical illusion. Imagine yourself looking at some large and splendid painting, but from a distance of three inches and through a powerful lens. You will see the details of brushwork and little else; and if you look closer with a still more powerful lens, you will just see a mess. In order to take in the picture as such, the full splendour of the artist's intention and achievement, you need to distance yourself, to stand some little way back from it.

By the standards of certain bad philosophies, you will then be 'romanticising' it. There is always the reductionist sense in which a great painting is nothing but chemicals smeared on canvas, in which a symphony concert is nothing but people being paid to make the air vibrate; and it's in that sense alone that Catholics are ordinary.

Only God perceives the fullness of what they are. But even from my own very insufficient viewpoint, I sometimes catch glimpses of it, if only at a rather pedestrian level. I am in fact prepared to go out on a limb and say that as a matter of experience—other things being equal —these ordinary Catholics show a marked tendency to be nicer and happier and wiser than other people. (But other things aren't always equal; and in any case, I have little social experience of the saints. They can be prickly and exacting and embarrassing to deal with, irascible like St. Jerome or neurotic like St. Alphonsus or socially disruptive like that famous streaker and drop-out St. Francis. If you invited St. Paul to dinner, do you think he'd add to the easy social fun of the occasion? Would the Lord?)

'Loving the Church': I find it surprisingly easy, and not only according to some picturesque vision of it that might be generated by ecclesiastical romanticism. By a kind of miracle, it can even make me feel humble: what have I done to deserve a place among such people?

But of course, there was never any question of deserving.

Even so, one's own Catholicism can be felt as a kind of

personal glory. Are such feelings dangerous? May one lawfully and prudently be proud of 'being a Catholic'?

In a certain sense, I think one may: we are citizens of no mean city.

When the Pope visited England in 1982, this fact was suddenly dramatised before the public eye. Old feelings had persisted, to the effect that 'being a Catholic' was an odd, furtive, hole-and-corner sort of thing. But in the carnival atmosphere of those few days, it was revealed as a participation in something large and splendid. Catholics held their heads a little higher: their non-Catholic friends spoke in a certain wistfulness, a certain envy.

Something large and splendid, and—most obviously —in the cultural and creative sense. One can point at the *Divine Comedy* and the Sistine Chapel, at the whole monumental achievement of Catholic Europe, and say "Yes, *we* did that." (But in order to be consistent, one must then be prepared to blush for Torquemada and for much else besides.)

It's the city's glory, not our own; and if we raise the question at a more spiritual level, we shall find little cause for conceit. We might even find cause for shame. Could it possibly be that we are the weak cases, given the fullness of Christ's Faith when others have to make do with much less, as a sick man might be given a particularly nutritious diet? We cannot expect to understand the purposes and providences of God. But there has to be some explanation—however invisible to ourselves—of the fact that most people don't have that fullness of Faith; and that might be it.

We have certainly no cause for spiritual pride. As

Catholics, we are complete or integral and in that sense 'perfect' Christians. But we cannot give ourselves airs on that account, despising others. It is not a matter of perfection in what we achieve: it is a matter of completeness in what we are given and what we are supposed to attempt and may in fact attempt very feebly.

If we need to be put in our place, this metaphor will help. Let us imagine two schoolboys who sit together for an examination, its rules specifying—as, I think, with the School Certificate of my younger days—that five subjects are compulsory. One boy is a brilliant scholar, but only in four subjects: he does no work at all on the fifth, not knowing that he must. The other boy is something of a dunce in all five, lazy too, but he does at least know the rules. In that sense, though in no other, he is the more learned of the two, or at least the better-informed: he is in a position to enlighten and correct his far cleverer friend, and charity obliges him to do so in ample time. But he is still an idle dunce. He may manage to scrape through in all five subjects or he may fail altogether, while the other boy soars in four and even (with the help of late nights and black coffee) in five.

It's a great thing to do well: knowing what needs to be done is only a prosaic necessity, no matter for pride. It's a real necessity for all that.

The question of Catholicity or completeness in one's Christian discipleship is closely related to the question of Christian unity: together, they add up to a subject which is—as the examiners used to say—"to be attempted by all candidates", not to an optional extra for the brilliant. But the Examiner is said to bend the rules in cases of genuine misunderstanding: he is also clever at distinguishing the dull boy who has really tried from the smart self-confident idler, and at treating both accordingly.

As we have seen, there is a perfectly legitimate subsense and usage which makes 'the Church' mean 'the clergy', the Pope and Bishops in particular. This raises a disconcerting possibility. If 'loving the Church' is a good thing, will we need to work up warm feelings towards ecclesiastical persons? The task would be easy enough in some cases, but difficult or impossible in others.

Fortunately for us, personal feelings are of little importance here. But as followers of Christ, we do need to have punctilious respect for his chosen representatives, his emissaries or apostles, and so for the key role played in the Church by its Apostolic Hierarchy.

That role seems to bother some people, and chiefly—I suspect—because it runs counter to certain prevailing obsessions in the egalitarian sense. The mere word 'Hierarchy' carries an immediate suggestion of some people being set over other people: it also suggests doctrinal authority, a possibility of our being told the answer when we'd prefer to choose our own.

Anything of that sort is of course unacceptable to men of this age. But, although stipulations in that sense are frequently made, they cannot be made without absurdity. Any man is free to say that there is no specific and definitive intervention of God within the historical process. But it is absurd to admit such an intervention, while requiring God to conduct it on lines congenial to the dominant political and social thinking of the late twentieth century. God may have his own ideas.

There are many further points at which the tradition

and teaching of the Church runs counter to the dominant secular thinking of our time. It then needs particularly firm and careful defence, by the Apostolic Hierarchy and by others too. But certain semi-Catholics see things the other way round: they take it for granted that at every such point of difference, it must be the Church that is wrong and needs to adapt itself.

This assumption of theirs strikes me as preposterous. Let us prescind altogether from divine revelation and the gift of faith: even then, the Catholic Church represents just about the largest body of coherent thought and experience that has ever existed. It has been around for a long time; it has engaged constantly with the basics of our condition: on the very lowest assessment, it must have picked up a great deal of empirical wisdom.

By contrast, the bulk of what we can sum up as 'modern thought'—the imprecision and insufficiency of that phrase being obvious enough—seems to me to have shallow roots and a certain thinness, a poverty of substance. Characteristically and often candidly, it is based upon philosophies of scepticism and negation: its exponents tend to be knowledgeable but to lack wisdom and even to deny the possibility of any genuine 'wisdom'. It is the thought of people who distrust thought, of bewildered people therefore, and it seldom does anything like justice to the complexity of this world and of our life and experience within it. The strictly scientific field is an obvious exception: empirical observation, the repeatable experiment made under controlled conditions—we're on firm ground there. But as soon as we move on to general interpretation, it starts to tremble underfoot.

Even from a position of religious neutrality, I'd regard

the Pope and the priests as far more likely to talk sense about the human basics than those who now claim—on the flimsiest of grounds—to know better.

Does this seem like just another instance of the intellectual arrogance for which Catholics are notorious? If so, a true story will show it in a different light.

The late E. F. Schumacher, author of *Small Is Beautiful*, was a truly remarkable man. During the 1970s, he was widely acclaimed as an inspired prophet for our age. His practical wisdom was immense, he was consulted by governments world-wide, and, while others were wringing their hands about poverty in the Third World, he worked out something that could actually be done about that grievous problem. I knew him well in his later years and am therefore in a position to outline the path that led him to the Catholic Church.

That path began at a curious point. Schumacher was Chief Economist to the National Coal Board in London, and the time came when he found himself in vehement opposition to its official policy. The people at the top had decided that the coal industry should be steadily run down, and that the country should make more and more use of imported oil. This struck Schumacher as insanity. The oil would run out much sooner than the coal, and, in any case, it had to be transported—vulnerably—from one of the most unstable regions in the world. *That* wasn't the right way to run practical affairs!

"Well", asked somebody, speaking in a wider sense, "What *is* the right way to run practical affairs?"

"A good question", said Schumacher; and not being able to answer it in general terms, he embarked upon a

wide course of reading, in the hope of finding practical
wisdom somewhere. He read everybody and everything:
Plato and Aristotle, Marx and Mao, Hitler and Gandhi,
all the philosophers and economists and political theorists
of East and West, of past and present, all with a completely open mind, ready to embrace practical wisdom
wherever it might be found, for his own good and for
that of the National Coal Board.

At one point, when so engaged, he was advised to
include in his reading the great social encyclicals put out
by the Popes of Rome from Leo XIII onwards.

"But why? The Popes may know all about religion,
but I'm not interested in that. Elderly celibates, living in
that ivory tower of the Vatican, won't know anything
about the practical conduct of temporal affairs; and that's
what I'm interested in."

"You read the social encyclicals, even so."

He did, and was astonished. Here, at last, was practical
wisdom! Here, at last, was good sense about the otherwise intractable problem of how to manage human
affairs in this life!

But where had those elderly celibates got it from?
Hardly from experience: they lived isolated in that ivory
tower, their eyes fixed upon eternity, and in the younger
days of each Pope, he had lived in priestly detachment
from the day-to-day worries of practical men.

This curious phenomenon needed some kind of explanation; and when Schumacher realised what this was
—not without the unnoticed help of what Catholics call
'grace'—he took the obviously consequential step.

"All roads lead to Rome." But was there ever another
road which, ending up at Rome, started with dissatis-

faction with the economic policies of a government agency?

How interesting it would be to walk a little further down Schumacher's road and discover that all Popes were invariably right about everything and that every priest resembled Chesterton's Father Brown, being possessed of a spiritual wisdom so intense that he could pierce at once to the heart of any conceivable problem!

What we actually find is something less than that, but something real none the less, sufficient to arouse the curiosity of any thinking person.

Here in England, the Catholic priest was an enigmatic figure for many years, often a sinister figure as well— the blandly smiling Jesuit, let us say, who went gliding secretly down corridors, knowing and manipulating all things, controlling the rise and fall of statesmen and empires, all to the Greater Glory of God. In *John Inglesant*, just such an archetypal figure was so staged as to influence many. A persistent archetype: in that version, it was eventually teased out of existence by Evelyn Waugh's preposterous 'Fr. Rothschild, S.J.'.

Papal Rome has often been seen in correspondingly romantic terms. One envisages those Cardinals, men of the type whose lips smile while their eyes do not, ascetic but epicurean too, men of patiently inflexible power, thinking always in terms of continents and centuries. It is said that a document once turned up in the Vatican archives upon which some such Cardinal had written, "This matter has been raised prematurely: let it be raised again in two hundred years' time."

That image of long-term remorseless efficiency may well have corresponded with the facts, or with some of them. But I cannot help remembering that Papal Rome was wholly run by Italians until recently, and still is to a very considerable degree; and in my experience, anything run by Italians is a kind of good-natured chaos, a matter of confused but cheerful improvisation that somehow works.

Somebody ought to write a new history of Papal Rome, re-interpreting the whole story in terms of that engaging fact.

A certain affectionate cynicism towards the clergy comes naturally to the Catholic mind. Waugh, a Catholic of the most fiercely traditional loyalty, always represented priests in some unflattering light. At the climax of *Brideshead Revisited*, the crucial role is played by a priest who is stupendously ordinary—a common man of very limited mentality, called in like a plumber or a carpenter to do a specific job, uninterested in the exalted rank of his dying penitent, and—it would seem—of no spiritual or other vision whatsoever. In what apocalyptically transcendent terms would Father Brown have spoken at that bedside? But Waugh was writing as a Catholic of some years' experience, whereas Chesterton—when, on the most tenuous sort of factual basis, he invented Father Brown—was not.

The phenomenon has fascinated many a novelist. A Ph.D. thesis for somebody: *Images of the Catholic Priest in English Fiction*.

Priests? I tend to like them, to find them good company; but only when they're personally at peace with the tradition and teaching of their Church. When they're in some state of unresolved inner conflict about it, as some are, they commonly strike me as tensed-up and even neurotic. This makes them rather difficult company.

For my part, I like to think of priests as coming in two varieties, differing slightly in function. There are thin priests and fat priests. It is the function of a thin priest to say: "Repent, for Judgment is not far distant! This life passes away, this world is but a shadow: wretched sinners that we are, we must fear the anger of God; we must work out our salvation in fear and trembling. Our adversary the Devil goes about like a roaring lion, seeking whom he may devour: only the utmost in austerity and devotion will save us from his clutches." It is the function of a fat priest to say: "The war is over, and our side has won! What a lovely world we live in, and how excellent its delights are when not spoiled by intemperance! Be happy and—above all—be grateful! And for Heaven's sake (literally), don't *worry*! God's love and forgiveness are immeasurably greater than our fiddle-de-dee little sins."

Both are right, of course.

Advice for any priest who reads this book: have an adaptable waistline. In the pulpit, be a thin priest: that's the place for stern warnings, for the inflexible assertion of principle, for putting the necessary fear of God into us. But in the confessional, be a fat priest: that's the place for extreme gentleness, for putting confidence and the even more necessary love of God into us.

Some of today's semi-Catholics are made uneasy by that word 'priest': it has such very sacral, sacrificial, and hierarchical overtones. They want that office and function to exist (if at all) in some more human and secular and egalitarian version. Instead of a sworn and anointed priest, standing at the altar to celebrate the Holy Sacrifice, we are now to see an ordinary man (or woman) who happens to preside over the Eucharistic assembly—an assembly that we are to see primarily in terms of togetherness or community. They tell us again and again that priesthood is a ministry of love and service.

The most obvious reply is that *all* Christian life should be a ministry of love and service. But it's also useful to remember how this particular ministry was seen by its Founder. It was to resemble the work of a farm labourer who gathers in the harvest, a fisherman who casts his net in hopes of a good catch, and a shepherd who looks after the stupid flock. As understood literally, such activities are useful indeed, but only for mankind and (as it were) unsymmetrically. If some articulate wheat-plant or fish or sheep were to be interviewed about such things, I do not suppose that 'love' or 'service' or 'community' would be the first words that occurred to him. He would be more likely to speak like a Marxist, complaining about this exploitation of the weak by the strong.

It is not to be supposed that the Lord chose his metaphors foolishly. Priests should certainly be kind and helpful people. But this fact should not be so emphasised as to obscure the sacral and magisterial nature of their office or the nature of their primary task, which is the exploitation of humanity in the interests of God.

Belloc said that while it's the mark of a Catholic culture to persecute the Church, it's the mark of a Protestant culture to tolerate it. In England and the United States, we certainly find nothing like the furious anti-Catholicism of Catholic Europe.

There is a kind of logic behind this seeming paradox. When judged by human standards, the Catholic clergy can appear more commendable in so far as one *disbelieves* their religion.

How can this be? Well, consider this proposition and premise: "The Catholic Faith is a tissue of nonsense and delusion from beginning to end." Given that premise, it follows that all the priests must be either fools or crooks: fools in so far as they actually believe all that nonsense, and crooks in so far as they pretend to believe it, and preach it to others, for the sake (presumably) of their own position and power. Then, when the sceptic actually meets some of them, he gets a pleasant surprise: they are so clearly not to be dismissed in terms of simple folly or crookedness. They prove much better than he expected, and he commends them.

Contrariwise, a fully-believed Catholic doctrine of Church and priesthood can easily generate extremely high expectations of what such men will be like. A priest is an *alter Christus*, another Christ, a presence and instrument of the Godhead among men: he is a man of total dedication, of holiness and poverty and simplicity, and his light shines before men. Such expectations are precariously founded. Nothing in Scripture or Catholic doctrine tells us anything about how well priests—or Bishops, or Popes—are likely to behave in practice; and it is as well to remember that in the persons of Judas the betrayer and Peter the denier, the original Apostolic College displayed a conspicuous failure-rate of nearly 16.7%, which cannot have been paralleled very often in later years. If we include Thomas the doubter or (briefly) the agnostic, the figure rises to 25%.

But where faith has led to high expectations at the

human level, it can suffer a rude shock if—as sometimes happens—the local priest turns out to be a bully, or a drunk, or a fool. A good Christian will forgive such failings in him and in all men. But he may still feel that his ideal of the Church has been betrayed by its official representatives; and so, while venerating the sacramental priesthood, he may become highly critical of actual priests, and even hostile to them. They, more than others, are so conspicuously not what they should be.

The roots of European anti-clericalism are more complex than that in fact. But in general, where men make high claims, they must expect to be judged by high standards. They can disappoint more easily than others.

But the failings of the clergy—the top-level clergy included—are not a simple negative: they provide a cynical-seeming but perfectly sound argument *in favour of* the Catholic Faith, as was seen by Abraham the Jew in Boccaccio's story, the second in the whole *Decameron*. The Church would have vanished from the world's scene a long time ago if good leadership and clerical perfection were what kept it in being.

A certain cynicism about the clergy is not confined to Catholics. But Swift was surely exaggerating when he said that he "never saw, heard, nor read that the clergy were beloved in any nation where Christianity was the religion of the country. Nothing can make them popular but some degree of persecution."

There may be something in that, but not much. My comment, however, would be that it isn't the clergy's job to make themselves beloved and popular. They follow a Master who was howled to his death by an angry mob.

Or they are supposed to follow him. In rural Gloucester-
shire, signposts used to be called 'clergymen' because
they pointed the way but didn't go along it themselves.
Then, during the Second World War, their inscribed
fingers were taken down so that they should offer no
guidance to the Nazi invader: only the posts remained,
and, since these had ceased even to point the way, they
were called 'bishops'.

Or so people say.

The clergy, the ecclesiastical institution, 'Rome' itself
—towards all that, a certain cynicism is appropriate but
a certain affection too, and a definite veneration. There's
an obvious danger if we confuse the means with the
end, the package with the product, the tickets with the
destination or even the journey. But for many people
of our time—the academic and literary intelligentsia
especially—the converse danger is, I suspect, more
immediate. There is such a thing as clerical Pharisaism.
But there is also an anti-clerical and anti-ecclesiastical
Pharisaism of the laity, and I have seen a great deal of
this. I see it as a mode of pride, a determination to
be on top, coupled with a deep-seated scepticism of the
intellect.

All is well so long as you love the Lord and—for his
sake—everything that you associate with him. As a
human institution and a cultural inheritance, the Church
can of course be valued for its own sake, even by an
unbeliever and not necessarily on aesthetic lines alone.
Charles Maurras was an atheist, though he made a good
end; and he saw the Church as inheriting the Roman
order, the Imperial discipline, and as constituting the
necessary backbone of all civilisation accordingly. His

associated political thought was more than merely ques-
tionable: none the less, given his unbelief, that was one
legitimate way of valuing the Church.

But more or less unconsciously, the believer can come
to give primacy to such considerations; and that's where
the danger comes in. If a man came to value the Lord
Jesus simply and solely as validating the beloved and
beautiful Church, he could hardly fail to be aware of the
fact—the idolatry, we might say. But one can proceed
some way along that road in considerable innocence,
unconsciously making Jesus into a means instead of a
Lord. He and his Church can seem so very *useful* for a
variety of purposes, social or cultural or political or
whatever they may be! What else can preserve the
threatened values of Western society? What other influence can make the degenerate young behave decently?
What else can save us from the Communist menace? In
an age of rootlessness and confusion, where else can we
find such a comforting sense of stability and continuity
and certainty, of deep roots in the Good Old Days?

The possibilities are many. Such secondary questions
may well be what draws a man's attention to the Lord
and his Church in the first instance: partial answers
to some of them will perhaps come thereafter, as by-
products of his discipleship. But the Lord will not
consent to be used as a means; and while his Embassy
here can rightly be loved, it is not the same thing as
our Homeland.

Even so, it's a bad sign when people hate it.

'Being a Catholic': yes, it does involve (among other
things) a certain relationship to a clerical institution;
and like a marriage, this relationship can sometimes be

difficult. But even at the worst, it was never quite what those people supposed who—forgetting the raw human condition—saw it from the outside and in quasi-political terms.

And it's only in close-up that this clerical institution appears to dominate the picture. Stand back, and you'll see something very different and quite extraordinary, a strange divine sea of redeemed humanity, an uncountable multitude of every place and every period, all standing before the Throne in white, carrying palms and singing —a life and hope and fragrance that pervades and trans-figures this world

> From where the western seas gnaw at the coast of Iona,
> To the death in the desert, the prayer in forgotten places
>   by the broken imperial column

and to every place and moment that now seems to us merely pedestrian, merely squalid, beyond the reach of any such poetry.

Nothing is beyond the reach of what we're talking about when 'being a Catholic' comes up for discussion. Its name is Resurrection.

Chapter Three

The Third Answer

'Being a Catholic': it means that we needn't lead "lives of quiet desperation" any more. We can lead lives of faith, hope, and charity instead; and there are senses in which I'd put the emphasis upon hope, which is in notably short supply nowadays, whereas there seems to be an abundance of generalised but bewildered goodwill.

Once upon a time, in the city of Stockholm, I met a sad Iranian, a Zoroastrian by background but now a kind of religious nihilist. When he learned that I was a Catholic, he rebuked me on curious lines.

"You Catholics are cruel people", he said; "You tell the truth, and you shouldn't do it. Truth is a harsh and painful thing and should be left unsaid: it's always kindest to leave people with their illusions."

That was the voice of his ancestry—if not precisely of Zoroaster himself, then of all those later and related cults that have denied the goodness of this world, this creation, and (in that sense) of reality and truth. How plausibly and attractively they spoke! The real is evil: only the ideal, even the imaginary is good.

Such ideas, although seldom so expressed, are extremely influential in our time: they add up to the primary point of difference between the Church and the present-day world. 'Being a Catholic' has many shades of meaning, many resonances: there's one rock–bottom sense in which it indicates an eccentric who still believes in the reality of truth and the goodness of reality.

That Iranian's words came close to echoing the voice of Dostoevsky's Grand Inquisitor, and the religious question they raised by implication is indeed an ultimate one—*the* ultimate one. How can we look with favour upon 'truth' and 'reality'? Is the universe really on our side? How can we possibly believe the first words of the Bible and the Creeds? Doesn't the despair of our raw condition mean that the Creator—if any—must be utterly unlike a loving and almighty Father?

It's all in the Book of Job.

My Iranian friend did at least take in something that eludes many—the fact that, as Catholics, we claim to be talking about truth, about objective reality, about how things actually are, about the facts of our raw condition and our redeemed condition as well.

I can understand any man denying the claim and saying that the truth is not as we suppose: with an effort, I can also understand the mind of the sceptic who says that there isn't any real 'truth'. But I'm baffled by those numerous people who can't really take in the fact that we make a claim of that objective sort—the ones who assume that we're talking about *feelings*.

I have encountered this assumption time and time again, even in well-read people who ought to know better. "So, as a Catholic, you feel . . .", "The Pope feels . . .", "Many present-day theologians feel . . .", and so forth.

Feelings, indeed! No responsible thinker can take them seriously; they prove no sufficient basis for either thought or action. My feelings are the fruit of my psychology, my childhood and education, my cultural conditioning: the state of my glands or my digestion can change them radically from one day to another. I wouldn't risk a penny on anything they told me. Yet all these people talk as though faith had no other basis and was therefore a blind and irrational thing.

A confession: if I did go by feelings, I wouldn't be a Catholic. I often feel that a Lutheran theology is more attractive and a Calvinist theology more plausible. But I have reasons for regarding both as un-Catholic—that is, as one-sided and therefore deceptive.

Spare my feelings!

But how can faith not be blind, when its Object lies beyond direct apprehension?

The answer might be that 'blindness' has two meanings, one relative and one absolute, as I discovered when I was learning to fly aeroplanes—an experience which gave me a most useful metaphor for the whole question of faith and reason and of 'feelings' in relation to both.

In normal flight, you keep an occasional eye on your instruments while orienting yourself principally by the horizon and the visible world below. (I am thinking of the days when aeroplanes *were* aeroplanes and had not yet become computerised projectiles.) Visual flight is thus a straightforward affair, and at a pinch and given a little experience, you could fly safely without any instruments at all—in good visibility, that is. But visibility isn't always good. Night or cloud can sometimes mean that there isn't any horizon or any visible world; so you have to learn 'blind flying'. They don't tear your eyes out or even blindfold you, but they do put you under an opaque hood, with nothing but your instruments to look at.

Now, it's the first principle of this art that feelings are highly deceptive. Some people used to speak of "flying by the seat of one's pants"—that is, by responsiveness to the gravitational and inertial pull of one's body in this direction or that, as experienced at the seat level. But that pull can fool you: it can make you feel that you're skidding to the right when in fact you're slipping or turning to the left. So a genuinely 'blind' pilot—and in wartime, one might suddenly become blind in mid-flight—would be out of control at once, and disastrously.

But so long as you are only relatively blind—engulfed in night or cloud, that is, but with good instruments clearly in view—you can manage perfectly well. The rough weather may toss your aircraft hither and yon, so generating a tumult of deceptive feelings in the seat of your pants. But you must repress or ignore these, making an act of blind faith in your instruments. So trusted, they will bring you through.

It isn't really 'blind' faith, of course. Your reasons for trusting them are perfectly rational. You have a sufficient understanding of how they work, though you need not be an expert on their manufacture and repair: when safely on the ground and under no stress, you could explain their reliability (and its limitations) in the most lucid manner. The theory of the matter is entirely clear.

But its practice, when you're flying blind in rough weather, is a psychologically different thing. Every nerve in your body may then scream out for reduced airspeed and left rudder when the exact opposite is needed, and you'll need every ounce of pure will-power if you're to retain faith in your instruments and so avoid a possibly disastrous spin. What you thereby achieve will feel at the time wholly irrational, as when one makes some kind of leap in the dark, some *acte gratuite* of pure faith. But, while the best logic in the world won't help you at such a moment, this will still be an act and victory of the will *as directed by the intellect*.

Catholic teaching amounts to a set of instruments, wholly reliable within their built-in limitations. They don't answer all possible questions. But they do represent the real state of affairs, they do tell you what you must think and do for survival when the time of darkness and upheaval comes—the time when you can't see a thing, when every instinct tells you (fatally) to do something else.

We wouldn't need those instruments if we were unfallen—not subject to the force of gravity—and always flew in perfect weather, through smooth and pellucid skies. But it was in the English climate that I learned to fly, not without scary moments; and this image of the relationship between feelings and faith and reason has haunted me ever since.

A turbulent sky in zero visibility—that's a "strange divine sea" if ever there was one: disastrous if you don't have instruments, most exhilarating if you do.

How does all this work out in practice?

We can envisage the Church as standing up in the world's marketplace and uttering (initially) just three loud shouts. The first of these is at the level of empirical reportage: "He is risen!" The second is at the level of theological interpretation: "This shows that he was and is the promised Messiah, the Son of God!" The third is in the imperative: "Repent, believe, be baptised in his name, and be saved!"

There are some who hear and obey. But there are

others who say "I don't believe it!"; and to them, the Church's reply is not "I can prove everything I've been saying", but "In that case, kneel humbly and ask God for the gift of faith."

There are some who take that good advice. But there are others who say "That would be a dishonest course of action, an exercise in auto-hypnosis or self-deception." There are many such people, and it's for their sake that the philosophical or argumentative method starts to be useful, despite its insufficiency and its irrelevance to the condition of others.

Faith is not the end-product of some chain of syllogisms: you cannot make yourself (or anyone else) into a believing Catholic by force of logic alone. Apologetics is a most necessary thing, but it isn't the art of proving Catholicism true. It's the art of refuting that last objection—of proving that, if a man does kneel humbly to ask God for the gift of faith, he is behaving in a highly realistic and rational manner, not dishonestly, not in some improper spirit of wilful self-deception and fantasy. There are some people to whom life and thought and suffering have made this fact obvious enough. But there are others who want to have it proved.

But how far is it capable of being proved?

In any enquiry, as Aristotle told us, we must expect only that kind of proof and certainty that is made possible by the nature of our subject-matter; and we may possibly be in too much of a hurry to say that religious subject-matter admits of practically no proof or certainty, and we will then end up as agnostics. But we shall then have missed the point. We were not talking about the substantive content of doctrine and theology: we were talking about realistic and rational behaviour, and its difference from every kind of self-deception and fantasy. There, we are on sufficiently familiar ground. We have encountered that difference in a number of fields, mostly unconnected with religious belief: we know reasonably well how to handle it, and we can usually find a sound basis for our practical decisions.

That's the level at which the Catholic apologist operates, that's the sense in which he 'proves' his case, and—at that level, in that sense—as rigorously as any logician or lawyer or scientist could desire. But when he's finished his task successfully, the kneeling and asking still needs to be done.

It can sometimes be done once and for all. But the Church never limited itself to those three initial shouts, those two assertions and that one command: what with 'the development of doctrine' and other factors, that cry of "I don't believe it!" can rise to one's lips again and again, perhaps throughout one's lifetime. Reasoned argument will sometimes help to silence it, but not always, and least of all where deep passions are involved, as they often are—for example—in any question involving sex or violence or pride. When the sky grows dark and turbulent, throwing the pilot into total reliance upon his instruments, one or more of those three factors will commonly be responsible.

For many of us, therefore, the humility of kneeling and asking is a lifelong burden. But it's never irrational, never unscientific: it's a high integrity of the mind.

'Orthodoxy' in our Catholicism, punctilious fidelity to the tradition and teaching of the Church: there are two mistakes that we can make about this.

The first is to think that it doesn't matter, having

somehow become obsolete: the second is to think that it's enough.

It does matter, rather as it matters for you to have a skeleton. But if you were hard bones and nothing else, you wouldn't be human.

Foundations are absolutely necessary for a house, but you can't live in them: a pilot needs to trust his instruments, but on their own account, they'll never lift him off the ground.

"But many present-day theologians feel that 'orthodoxy', in that sense of the word, has simply ceased to be meaningful and relevant!"

No doubt; but what of it? Our Faith is something "that comes to us from the Apostles": it isn't a matter of what theologians feel, and it would be wholly shifting and amorphous if it were. (Read: it is wholly shifting and amorphous where it is.)

The following words ought to be inscribed, in ten-inch letters of gold and fire, around the walls of every large room in which Catholics foregather—every cathedral and church, and (especially) the main lecture-hall of every seminary: THE NORM OF CATHOLIC TRUTH, IN FAITH AND MORALS, IS NOT TO BE FOUND IN CURRENTLY FASHIONABLE PATTERNS OF THEOLOGICAL SPECULATION.

The words "fashionable" and "speculation" are there intended in the fully adversative sense of each.

"But you Catholics have to believe what you're told to believe! You aren't allowed to think for yourselves!"

Such accusations are frequently brought, even today, and they baffle me in two distinct ways.

In the first place, how can you possibly "think for yourself" in transcendentally religious matters without ending up as an agnostic? Logically speaking, the existence of God can be inferred from the experienced fact of his creation: so, perhaps, can the immortality of the soul. But where do we go from there, and—if the word 'think' is to be used rigorously—*how*? Nothing is easier than the religious hunch, guess, or opinion: one may also claim to have had something in the way of religious 'experience', though in the absence of external confirmation of some kind, psychological considerations must always cast a certain doubt upon this. But how are we to 'think' in any more solid sense of the word? Let it be granted that we have the utmost in scholarship and philosophical subtlety: given some transcendental question in faith or morals, how are we to reason our way to a sound and well-supported answer?

I'm afraid that when people speak of 'thinking for oneself' in matters of religion, they are seldom recommending anything more than unqualified reliance upon one's own hunches and guesses and opinions, together with one's own interpretation of such religious 'experiences' as may have come one's way, and with mere fashion likely to play a crucial role in practice. Each man will then be his own oracle, or each group or each generation: many versions of 'truth' will thus be apprehended, none of them better or worse than the others.

Many people appear to think like that: they should properly be called agnostics.

I am further baffled by those who see Catholic Faith as a matter of simple command-and-obedience, very much like the Guards on parade. The Pope (or it might be a Council) barks out the word of command: "Believe so-and-so!" And all these millions of Catholics world-wide, being trained like Guardsmen in the habit of instant obedience, do what they're told: they immediately start believing so-and-so.

This idea has always struck me as a psychological absurdity: how can one possibly believe anything by an act of the pure will, of simple obedience to orders? We all know that governments and similar agencies can control the outward expression of unwelcome beliefs: they can censor the press, they can silence the dissident. We also know that within limits, people can be *caused* to believe this or that by means of brainwashing and hypnosis and similar techniques. But how can any individual or agency *command* belief? Let us suppose that you are most willingly enrolled in some tightly-disciplined organisation: your dedication is absolute, you seek only to obey. Let us now suppose that the competent authority tells you to believe something that you don't already believe. How do you set about the task of obeying? What psychological contortions do you attempt?

The 'act of faith', as understood by Catholics, is not of that kind and would be impossible (as far as I can see) if it were. Its nature can be illustrated by reference to two familiar experiences. The first is what happens when we trust a reference book or some other source of information. It enlightens but it does not command. If we consult it, we shall sometimes discover a need to correct our previous thinking, and we shall do so if we are wise. But we can always close the book in irritation and retain our delusions.

Then, at a far deeper level, there is the experience of responding positively to a personal appeal for trust: "Please believe me! I know what I'm talking about!"

Here again, one can turn away in irritation and retain one's own preferred ideas. If the appeal for trust is well justified, one will then be preferring delusion. But one will also be damaging a personal relationship, and this may be a far more serious matter. One is sometimes asked to make an 'act of faith' in the doctor, and this can be difficult, since what he says about one's symptoms will not always be what one wants to hear: one can always tell him to go to Hell. This will be medically imprudent, but if it damages a personal relationship, little harm will be done: one can always find another doctor. It's otherwise with the trust that is asked and given within a happy marriage; and it's very much otherwise with the trust that is asked—through his Church—by Jesus. Any refusal of that trust, any stubborn retention of one's own different and preferred thinking, will certainly mean delusion. But one's blood ought to run cold at the damage then done to the ultimate in personal relationships.

'Faith' was never a matter of simple obedience to some quasi-military word of command. It's a matter of trusting a person in the first instance, and so (to speak very broadly and crudely) of regarding a certain source of information as reliable, whereas one's own hunch or guess or opinion must always be very unreliable indeed —almost as unreliable as the present-day climate of opinion.

Faith–as–information: the very idea sets some people's teeth on edge. Surely 'faith', to be authentic, has to be a matter of shared experience?

Well, it's certainly that as well. But, unless it's information as well and primarily, the evangelical or missionary task is going to become absurdly proud. There's nothing inherently proud in claiming to have information which others do not possess. Let us imagine a group of people, expert in world politics, who are discussing the international scene. Embarrassed by my own ignorance, I tiptoe out of the room and switch on the radio elsewhere; and I then hear a startling news-flash, of sharp relevance to what those experts were discussing. I am guilty of no pride if I then return and confound them all with this new information.

Faith-as-information says to the world: "We've been told something that you need to know!" But faith-as-shared-experience says to the world: "Be like us! Feel as we do!" The former message may well be received with doubt. But the latter message is going to seem like a mode of pride or arrogance: it is likely to be received with irritation.

Here as elsewhere, countless Catholics are sharply at variance with the tradition and teaching of their Church: countless others respond by retreating into a blindly rigid traditionalism. How should one strike a balance? Where should we draw the line?

One good formula: ". . . and of course, this means that practically all Catholics have been radically mistaken about this since the very beginning." When the thing said entails *that* consequence—and it frequently does—it can safely be rejected or ignored.

"But isn't it very arrogant of you Catholics to claim that your Faith has some kind of absolute rightness? There are a great many of you, of course, but your Faith is still a minority-thing: most people don't agree with you!"

The trouble is that every possible attitude to the religious question is a minority-thing. At one extreme, we find the man who simply couldn't care less about that question: he pays it no attention. Close to him we find the old-fashioned Logical Positivist who declares all religious questions to be meaningless: a little further on, we find the sceptic or agnostic maintaining—far more plausibly—that while religious questions have sufficiently clear meanings, they are incapable of being answered in this life. From there, you can move right across the board in any direction you like: at the other extreme you will find total commitment to faith and observance and dedication—Catholic here, Protestant there, Jewish or Moslem or Hindu elsewhere. But statistically speaking, each of these, from the one extreme to the other, is a minority-thing.

Whatever you think about religious matters, you have to come to terms with the fact that most people don't agree with you. It may be a distressing fact, but it isn't an important fact otherwise: it neither proves nor disproves anything at all.

"But don't you believe that the Holy Spirit speaks in the inmost heart of every man, and especially of every Christian?"

I certainly do. The trouble is that other voices speak there as well. Some of these will be relatively innocent, originating in nothing worse than one's psychology, one's social conditioning, one's education, one's class-interest, and so forth. But the Spirit of the Age may speak there also, prompting some to irrational assent and others (myself perhaps included) to an equally irrational contradiction: either way, it can cause the Holy Spirit to get shouted down. The same goes for more sinister voices—that of one's own pride, for example, one's intellectual conceit, to look no lower. And then there's always the silly random chatter of the mind.

Ideally, one should be able to distinguish these voices. But that of the Spirit is very easily faked by his competitors, and introspection provides no reliable way of telling the difference. Vehement feelings of certainty prove nothing.

In lesser matters, I often have vehement feelings of certainty and soon find them mistaken. "How extraordinary!" I then say; "I could have sworn that. . . !"

"Just as well you didn't", says my wife dryly; "Perjury is a sin and a crime."

But what about ecumenism? the brotherhood of all Christians, the reunion of the Churches?

Jacques Maritain once told Jean Cocteau that in all serious matters, we need to have soft hearts and hard heads. Cocteau's answer is not on record as far as I know, which is a pity: it might have been amusing, as might any conversation between two such dissimilar men. In my time, I have witnessed attempts at communication between Kenneth Tynan and C. S. Lewis, who spoke almost as though they were members of different species. It must have been rather like that with Maritain and Cocteau.

But the point was a good one; and so far as the reunion of the Churches is concerned, the work of the soft hearts is well advanced. We might even say that it nears completion. A visual impression in that sense was certainly given in 1982, when we saw the Pope and the Archbishop of Canterbury kneeling to pray, side by side, in the place of Becket's martyrdom.

But the work of the hard heads has scarcely begun. It is frustrated by a most powerful taboo—rather as when some shy and modest girl finds it impossible to mention her intimate symptoms to the doctor. So long as she does, he can't help her.

There is no hope of healing a divided Christendom unless the nature and causes of the sickness are faced in all candour and freely discussed in all charity. That means that we shall need to use two key six-letter words, 'heresy' and 'schism'. But those words are now deemed as improper as certain four-letter words were until recently: one simply does not utter them in polite company. They outrage the spirit of ecumenism.

They are of course controversial words. But then, 'the reunion of Christendom' is an inherently controversial subject. You cannot attach any coherent meaning to that expression which will not be controversial in itself and (in that sense) un-ecumenical. Ecumenism is a good cause: Christian unity is a good cause. But they are different and even antithetical causes: in so far as you work for one, you work against the other.

How many pious heads now batter themselves silly against that brick wall!

"But the Inquisition. . . ."

It always intrudes itself into the argument at one point or another, as the ghost of something that happened a long time ago but is still alive in principle. Catholic churchmen no longer connive actively in the burning of heretics to death. But they once did so; and don't they still retain the central doctrine and mind-set which once made that seem a wholly righteous course of action?

The lamest possible reply: "Well, 'Inquisition' only means 'enquiry', or what the Americans call 'due process': it refers to nothing more than getting one's facts right. We don't want anyone treated as a heretic unless he actually is a heretic, do we?"

"Of course we don't; but that misses the entire point, and well you know it. Let's assume, for the sake of argument, that there is such a thing as 'heresy'—that a man can be mistaken in matters of religious belief. Anyone can be mistaken about anything, after all. But when we are honestly mistaken about something, we're only guilty—at the worst—of an intellectual failing: we haven't committed a sin, we haven't committed a crime, and we certainly haven't committed the awful sort of crime that might call for draconian punishment!"

Old memories linger, still generating distrust of rather that sort, whatever changes there have recently been in the visible patterns of Catholic behaviour. Current policies may indeed be open and ecumenical, discipline may indeed be easier. But beneath all that, isn't the Catholic Church still a tyranny of the mind?

A nourishment of the mind, one might prefer to say. An infringement of freedom? Only in an extremely strained sense. Feed a hungry man and you take away his freedom to go on being hungry. But that doesn't make you into a tyrant.

And in any case, who is in a position to cast the first stone? Catholic churchmen have been guilty of atrocious cruelty from time to time. But when the most has been made of all that, is the Church's record one-twentieth as bloody as that of the State, or of humanity in general? As I write, it is the declared policy of Her Majesty's Government—supported by all sensible and patriotic people—to burn certain foreigners to death by the millions, if and when their government does something sufficiently uncongenial to ourselves. We couldn't propose such things in the past: we didn't have the equipment, the know-how. But we did our best. As a Catholic, I must certainly blush for much of what that word 'Inquisition' suggests, even though the scale of that cruelty was—by modern standards, and in relation to the populations involved—microscopic. But I was a member of the organisation that did the Dresden bombing. Have I any less need to blush for that?

All of us have the whole filthy human record to blush for.

No, I don't want to see heretics burned at the stake. But then, I don't want to see *anybody* burned at the stake. (My feelings—for what feelings are worth—might be different if I had grown up in a wholly lawless and violent and barbarian society and were now among its victims.)

In all the horrors that we have in mind when we speak of the Inquisition, there was a central kernel of rightness. This is analogous to something that now finds expression in the law of most countries—in what we call the 'Trade Descriptions Act', for example. This is the law which, in England, obliges you to label goods accurately when you put them on the market: you must not package up some tough elderly horse-meat and sell it as prime Scotch beef. The principle of the totally free market is thereby infringed but—I think—justifiably. Only an extreme follower of Adam Smith and Milton Friedman would object, in principle, to prosecutions and even punishments under that Act.

"But you can't apply that principle to religious questions!"

On sceptical or relativistic premises, of course you can't—that is, if we start off by asserting dogmatically that religious truth is non-existent or unavailable or unimportant. But what if our present condition is more fortunate? Suppose that there is such a thing as a one-and-only answer to the human problem, a one-and-only escape-route from the human mess and despair: what are we then to say and do about those who falsify this?

As things now stand, many prosecutions might justly be brought under the Faith Descriptions Act. In that marketplace, there's a great deal of deceptive labelling.

We are told too often that 'faith' is more than a mere intellectual assent to doctrinal propositions. It's certainly much more than that: it's never less than that.

Those propositions stand to the divine Reality very much as a map stands to real countryside. Nobody confuses the two. But we travel in the dark, with the Reality beyond our direct apprehension, so we need a good map as we journey through life. A *good* map: reliable, as informative as may be, and with *terra incognita* clearly marked as such.

People sometimes ask why Catholics are so pernickety about points of doctrine. It would be one answer to say that one needs to be pernickety about maps, especially if one is going to depend on them. Once again, a military analogy may help. Our troops are advancing in the dark across very difficult terrain, harassed by enemies, and it would be all too easy for them to get lost, and worse. So the Army supplies them with maps, and it takes extreme care to see that they are accurate maps, unlike some that are on the market.

If the troops are caused or allowed to get hold of inaccurate maps, they will be put unnecessarily at risk; and this danger will still be present and equally serious, no matter whether the inaccuracies in question stem from well-meaning ignorance, or from laziness or incompetence, or from positive malice.

It might be better for those troops to have no maps at all than to be given false confidence by maps that deceived them.

"But isn't religious liberty a most sacred absolute? Didn't the Second Vatican Council concede as much, after so many centuries of intellectual tyranny on the Church's part? Isn't every man entitled to believe what he likes?"

Yes and no. As before society and the State, he must certainly enjoy religious liberty: he must be subject to no coercion. But as before God and his own conscience, he is absolutely obliged to conform his mind to apprehended reality, to face the facts, to live mentally in the real world. To believe 'what you like' is to let your thought be governed by preference: it has sometimes been called 'wishful thinking', and it is a prime sin of the intellect.

The Second Vatican Council re-asserted the ancient purpose, which was and is that all men should come to Christ in the fullness of his Church's Faith and Life. It recognised—none too soon—that governmental or similar coercion is a very bad way of seeking that end. But it gave no endorsement whatever to such concepts of 'religious liberty' as imply that one man's belief is as good as another—that operational maps can be drawn to whatever pattern takes your fancy, or that there are no real maps at all.

"One man's belief is as good as another's": if taken seriously, such words mean that all beliefs are objectively valueless.

And while error—the fact of being mistaken or wrong about something—can rightly be called a fault or failing of the intellectual sort, can it never include an element of moral impropriety as well?

Let us imagine Albert Einstein in mixed company upon some social occasion. Up comes a schoolboy and asks the great man to explain Relativity in a few sentences. Einstein hesitates: how can he put his highly abstract and mathematical theory into words that this boy will understand? He can only do his best. The fullness of that theory cannot possibly be put across, but he may at least be able to eliminate some of the more obvious misunderstandings of it, such as the schoolboy may have picked up from the popular press.

"Yes, yes, Dr. Einstein, that's all very interesting, and I can see what you mean about time being relative to different observers; but I think you're quite wrong about the curvature of space. Now, what *I* say is that. . . ."

A free country: let nobody challenge that boy's legal right to the expression of his own beliefs! But let nobody deny the fact that he's behaving like a fool and—what's worse—a most arrogant and ill-mannered sort of fool.

Intellectual error can be innocent enough. But assertive dogmatising beyond one's competence is never innocent:

in schoolboy or in professor, it's always an assertion of the naked ego, a sin of pride.

It may turn out one day, of course, that Einstein was wrong and that schoolboy right about the curvature of space. But the boy's rightness will then be accidental and unearned: his offence will remain.

No similar possibility arises in connection with God's attempt to reveal and explain himself to man. He may turn out to have been misunderstood: he cannot turn out to have been mistaken.

The ambiguities of 'faith'!

As a public speaker in the Catholic cause, I have sometimes found myself admired and even envied for that virtue, that gift. "It's a great thing to see a man taking a firm stand for what he believes in!"

For what *I* believe in? But if it was that, a firm stand for *my* preferred way of seeing things, would it be anything more than a great big ego-trip on my part? an attempt to force Derrickism upon others?

A variant of that same snare: I give my lecture or whatever it may be, and afterwards somebody comes up to congratulate me—a housewife or a Cardinal or somebody like that. "How wonderful it is to see such firmness in the Faith!"

Well, yes—so long as it really is that. But it could be something subtly different. Once again, consider this proposition: "The Catholic Faith is nothing but a tissue of nonsense and illusion from beginning to end." Given that premise, this conclusion follows: "Christopher Derrick has been making a stupendous fool of himself for many years." But this is absurd, since I'm Me and cannot possibly be a stupendous fool: *ergo*, the premise has to be erroneous.

The temptation naturally takes care not to present itself to one's consciousness as crassly as all that. But its subtler forms are a constant danger.

The theological gift of faith is not at all the same thing as the psychological quality of confidence. I have known wise and holy men, priests and prelates included, who possessed the former but not the latter. But confidence frequently disguises itself as faith, so as to deceive (if possible) even the elect.

It is possible, of course, to have both.

All men need some kind of hope to live by. But that theological gift of faith, where given and received, effects a transformation upon 'hope' as commonly understood.

I once met an old nun who had spent her entire working life as a missionary in China. She and a few others went out there in the 1920s, and over many years —in a rather remote place, I gathered—they brought their mission into existence: a clinic, an orphanage, a school, and a small chapel for themselves and for any possible converts. These were unlikely to come quickly: the Chinese are tough nuts for any missionary to crack.

Time passed and the mission prospered, hardly touched by the country's domestic and foreign wars. By now the nuns were well known locally and highly esteemed: they even had grounds for believing that they might make their first convert before long. But then, in 1949, the Communists suddenly came. They were polite but firm: twenty minutes to pack one small suitcase each, and then *out*.

A truck took them to Hong Kong, and from there they went back to England, which is where I met this particular nun. She sat there under an apple tree and told me this story: a brown and wizened old lady, perfectly serene, just waiting to die.

"But how terrible! Didn't it break your heart to see your entire life's work destroyed in a moment, with absolutely nothing to show for it?"

She smiled peacefully. "What did God give us blood for, if not to be poured out on the altar?"

It isn't Christian to be future-oriented in any serious way, to think in terms of achievement and results. Jesus of Nazareth was a kind of failure, and humanly speaking, he didn't make any perceptible mark upon history. (It was his followers who did that.)

If there were to be hope for the temporal future, its basis would need to be religious, in some minimal sense at least: we would have to work for a situation in which all men saw this life as a journey, never as being or including a destination. I suspect that this view of things would do more than anything else to abate their quarrelsomeness.

How peacefully fellow-travellers get along together, accepting one another as such! Consider airline passengers, for example: there should be a systematic study of their social behaviour, a mini-sociology of their relationships in the short-lived society, even the 'nation' which they constitute when airborne. They are all so friendly to one another! When earthborne, they will mostly be indifferent strangers. They may even be rivals, competitors, enemies: this flight may well have both Jew and Arab on board, both Greek and Turk, both conservative and socialist, and their hatreds will take over once again after the eventual baggage-claim. But now, as we drone along in this tin tube, we are all brothers.

How it would improve our behaviour if we all came to see this life as a shared journey!

But to what destination? To the grave, certainly; whereas airline passengers usually do arrive safely. Would they still behave as brothers if their journey was a hopeless one, having no real destination at all?

Would they then enjoy it? "To travel hopefully is a better thing than to arrive"; and I at least feel a certain sadness every time the engines quieten and we start our let-down from that sunlit blue-and-white Paradise, that strange divine sky, back to this too-familiar human world.

But how far can Stevenson's observation be pressed? We might still be able to travel enjoyably if we knew that arrival was going to be a sad disappointment, a literal let-down, even a zero. But could we still travel *hopefully*?

The great mistake is to suppose that 'eternity' means a further and now unlimited supply of time.

What Christians call 'hope' is very unlike any kind of temporal optimism: it is oriented towards something which we can only imagine as a future but is not a simple future in fact. We live in and for the present, "the point at which time touches eternity", and in considerable detachment from the temporal future.

> He who bends to himself a Joy
> Doth the winged life destroy;
> But he who kisses the Joy as it flies
> Lives in Eternity's sunrise.

Thus a holy man could write a book called *The Sacrament of the Present Moment*. As with that other spiritual classic called *Abandonment to Divine Providence*, you don't need to read the book: in each case, the whole message is there in the title.

It's by God's mercy that we don't know the temporal future.

Practical wisdom from Dunbar:

> Man, please thy Maker, and be merry,
> And give not for this world a cherry.

But if you don't give a cherry for your neighbours in this world, you won't be pleasing your Maker.

Death is what makes for despair: Resurrection is what makes for hope.

Spring is the season of renewal and new life, which is why Easter has to be a springtime festival. How do those people manage who, living in the southern hemisphere, make it into an autumnal festival? (If it comes to that, I don't see how Australian children can read English poetry, when such a word as 'April' means something totally different for them. "O for a beaker full of the warm North"?)

Every year, as the Paschal season comes round, we receive liturgical reminders that Jesus is—above all—the conqueror of death. That's where the Church puts the initial emphasis.

> *Mors et vita duello*
> *Conflixere mirando:*
> *Dux vitae mortuus*
> *Regnat vivus.*

"But we still have to die!" Not exactly: in him, we only have to 'die'. Those quotation marks signify a radically altered meaning.

Without him, of course, we are left to die, left in sin as well; and (if a four-letter word may be permitted) sin + death = Hell.

Of all the attempts that have been made to devise 'a Christianity acceptable to modern man', the silliest are those which try to dodge round the doctrine of Hell. Let the Lord's words be as figurative and culturally-conditioned as you like, let *sheol* and *Gehenna* be defined and distinguished with all possible subtlety: what remains, unmistakably and inescapably, is the urgency with which he spoke, as though each individual faced the real and imminent possibility of an absolute doom, a final disaster of the most personal kind, however this might need to be defined.

He offered Good News, but never under any rubric of "It's all right! You can relax, there's nothing to worry about!" His mere tone of voice rules that out, however we gloss particular texts: it was always "You're in a hell of a mess, but I can get you out of it *if* you do exactly what I say"—as with that fireman and the dilatory philosopher.

The whole doctrine of Hell is summed up in his famous threat "Ask and you shall receive." Or, as one might say with an inappropriate suggestion of inflexible destiny, "You get what's coming to you."

Asking or choice *versus* destiny: that ancient philosophical and theological teaser finds an occasional echo in common speech. Imagine some man whose behaviour eventually causes you to punch him on the jaw and send him flying. "You've been asking for that for a long time!" you snarl as he lies gasping.

Asking? In a way, yes.

Heaven is populated by those who said "Thy will be done" to God: Hell is populated by those who asked and even compelled God to say "All right, *your* will be done, if that's how you want it!"

Heaven is where you get what you always wanted: Hell is where you get your own way.

One should be very careful about asking for things: one might get them.

Prayer is of course difficult, not to say impossible. "I throw myself down in my chamber, and I call in, and invite God, and his Angels thither, and when they are there, I neglect God and his Angels, for the noise of a fly, for the rattling of a coach, for the whining of a door." Donne's sad confession will strike an answering chord in the memory of anyone who has ever tried to pray.

But things may not look so bad from above. It is doubtlessly true that we often suppose ourselves to be praying when we are really doing nothing of the kind: it is so easy to address one's own super-ego while supposing that one addresses God. But the converse may sometimes be equally true: our best moments of prayer may possibly be those that come and go inadvertently, unrecognised as such by ourselves.

Liturgy helps: it carries you along, especially (in my case at least) when most archaic and sacral, speaking most clearly of the Timeless. I find it a distraction in desacralised and casual versions—even an occasion of sin.

When we do manage to pray, we are (among other things) surfacing mentally into the real world. There, we are never alone—which is good news when we are sad and seek company, but bad news when we feel wicked and don't want to be watched.

In the pretend-world that we make for ourselves, of course, God is a nicely theoretical construction of the mind, something abstract and safely distant. He and his Mother and all the saints live in a remote Heaven, some eighteen hundred thousand million light-years away. This delusion enables us to feel as we did when—in my Air Force days—we were sent to some small out-station. Here, we can relax: distant Headquarters won't notice what we get up to!

But what if God turned out to be much closer to you than anything else—even closer than the experience of consciousness?

An unsettling thought, or perhaps a comforting thought.

In the course of what he called his "spiritual Aeneid", Ronald Knox—being on the verge of conversion, and therefore of a painful break with "loved surroundings and familiar friendships"—felt a certain sense of desolation and loneliness; and having recourse to a kind of *sors Vergiliana*, he came upon the words *maria undique, et undique caelum*, "sea and sky everywhere around me". But his scholar's mind saw that those words could be taken differently, though by nothing more than a kind of pun, in terms of Mary and Heaven. "Perhaps I was not so lonely after all."

It is not always easy for others to understand the place, the *kind* of importance that Catholics give to the Mother of Jesus. For all his Ulster Protestantism, C. S. Lewis came fairly close to an apprehension of this. "The Roman Catholic beliefs on that subject are held not only with the ordinary fervour that attaches to all sincere religious belief, but (very naturally) with the peculiar and, as it were, chivalrous sensibility that a man feels when the honour of his mother or his beloved is at stake. It is very difficult so to dissent from them that you will not appear to them a cad as well as a heretic."

James Morris came closer, I think, in this account of a Madonna and Child in the cathedral of Torcello, near Venice. "There are tears on her mosaic cheeks, and she gazes down the church with an expression of timeless reproach, cherishing the Child in her arms as though she has foreseen all the years that are to come and holds each one of us responsible."

What a remarkable prayer the *Hail Mary* is! It grasps the nettle, it asserts the central Christian paradox, the reversal of natural values: we address a Mother who saw her Son tortured to death, and we tell her that she is the most blessed or fortunate of all women. It also means that every Catholic grows up from childhood with three facts constantly upon his lips, facts about the human condition which others leave mostly unverbalised—the fact of his mortality, the fact of his sin, and the fact that he can't save himself but needs to be prayed for.

The remorseful love of Catholics for that Mother, and their cult of the saints in general, used to incur much Protestant rebuke and may still do so in some quarters. But I find it hard to sympathise with such rigour. What kind of a human love would it be that said, "I love *you*, but I refuse to speak to your mother or to your best and closest friends"?

Once again, love concentrates upon its object and

therefore—with no deflection or diminution—upon whatever or whoever is associated with that object, and in the measure of its close association.

Every saint is a case in point, and so—on slightly different lines—is your far-from-saintly neighbour.

"I love humanity—it's people I can't stand!" Those are the words of (I think) Lucy in *Peanuts*, that most theological of comic strips, and there can be few consciences that they fail to touch.

Television and the other media seem to me to have imposed a subtle falsity upon current notions of 'charity'. They bring the whole world's agony before our eyes, the sufferings of 'humanity' rather than of people, and we are thus predisposed to the great fallacy of global solutions while being also thrown into despair: what can we *do*?

How passionately we want that question to be an answerable one! How impatient we are with the limitations of practical action, the fact that we can't always *do* things about things!

Humanity suffers: that is to say, there are suffering people everywhere. This has always been true, and it will remain true in any foreseeable future. By our humanity, and by our Christianity even more, we are obliged to mitigate individual and local suffering to the best of our ability. But individual and local miseries are quite enough for us and are in fact all that we can take: we were never designed to cope, practically or emotionally speaking, with the troubles of an entire planet and an entire species. It's usually a mistake to try. When its task is conceived globally, charity soon ceases to be charity and becomes manipulation: it also displays a marked tendency to fail.

"Let us feed this hungry child, if only for a few weeks": Yes. When that opportunity presents itself, it must never be neglected.

"Let us establish an international organisation to stamp out world poverty and hunger": No. It is most unlikely to succeed. You will get your organisation going all right. But it will soon make a moral transition of the most subtly fatal sort: it will stop doing things *for* people (which is heavenly) and start doing things *to* people (which is hellish). In the event, its chief beneficiaries will be bureaucrats, airlines, hotels, and (most gloriously) the manufacturers of paper.

This world and the future of the human species are not in our hands. They're in God's hands if there is a God and in no possible hands if there isn't. Doing this or that is seldom the answer. When the Lord set out to save the world, he did so in the passive voice, not the active. His short life was certainly a busy one, and some people hold him forth as—primarily—the ideal practitioner of 'good works'. But those miracles of healing and feeding made no perceptible difference to the totality of sickness and hunger, and they were hardly intended to do so: they served as theological pointers rather than as humanitarian exertions.

It's by his accepted suffering that we are saved.

You were never told to love humanity: you were only told to love your neighbour, the first person you come across. Charity, to remain itself, needs to be specific. "He who would do good to another must do it in Minute Particulars", said Blake; "General good is the plea of the scoundrel, hypocrite, and flatterer."

"No, I don't believe that Jesus was God: I think he was just a very good man." A profoundly silly interpretation: yet it still gets offered.

A very good man? Let us imagine that I am somehow the possessor of powers that seem miraculous: I can feed the hungry, I can heal the sick and the insane, I can even raise the dead. We need not specify the exact nature of these powers. They may or may not be technically 'miraculous': either way, they make me—potentially— into the greatest benefactor mankind has ever known.

Given a humanitarian order of priorities, given a presumption that suffering is the worst of all evils, they impose a clear duty upon me; and if I am even a mildly good man, I shall not neglect this duty. I shall devote my life to the fullest possible use of these powers. Locally at first but then more widely, I shall see that the hungry *are* fed and that the sick *are* healed. (Shall I also contrive a general abolition of death and so of bereavement? Most people might call for this, but readers of Swift might hesitate.) If possible, I shall also pass these powers on to others, so causing all human existence to be trans- formed everywhere. But even if I can't do that, there's a tremendous amount that I will be able to do in the course of a long and dedicated life; and I will naturally get respect and all possible assistance from those in authority.

What will be your judgment upon me if, having these powers, I only use them in a small and almost perfunctory way, chiefly in order to draw attention to myself and to some special privilege and destiny of my own? if I challenge the authorities and so get into trouble, so that my early death terminates even those modest efforts? if I do train followers, but not primarily (or very effectively) in this humanitarian relief of suffering?

Your judgment can only be adverse. It's an old

observation. *Aut Deus aut malus homo*: the purposes and priorities of Jesus were clearly not what we would consider 'humanitarian', and if he wasn't God, we have to see him as a *bad* man—shockingly irresponsible in the use of these strange powers, full of delusions about his own importance, and in fact mad with pride.

But can we really see him like that?

We are stuck with a kind of paradox and must do full justice to both sides of it. By our Faith, humanitarian efforts and the relief of suffering are made *more* urgent, not less urgent. But at the same time, those things aren't the name of the game: they aren't what Christ and Christianity are all about. If they were, the hermit would be a culpable drop-out; whereas the Catholic mind has always seen his as a rare but real vocation to supreme holiness.

Human suffering comes in many different versions; and the political and economic preoccupations of today dispose us to attach particular importance to those versions of it that may be summed up as 'social injustice'. This undoubtedly exists, and we must try to ease it wherever we can. But we must not expect too much. Most attempts at 'the just society' only succeed in altering the pattern of injustice, often for the worse. We should never forget that Communism started off as a seemingly *good* idea. But in fact, the only good revolution is that *metanoia* to which we are called by Christ and his Church.

What does the voice of Christ say to the poor and the rich?

To the poor, whose characteristic sins are envy and anger: "Patience! Love your enemy, forgive those who trespass against you! It's when you suffer poverty and injustice and oppression that you come closest to me!"

To the rich, whose characteristic sins are pride and avarice and gluttony and hardness of heart, also anxiety: "Careful! At the best, you're making a dangerous mistake: at the very probable worst, you are living in sin and on the high road to Hell!"

For a good man, one great danger is that love of the poor can so easily rot into hatred for the rich. A millionaire is not to be presumed guilty in the sight of God, or a poor man innocent: camels do go through the eyes of needles, and his denial of this was one of the things that got Pelagius into trouble with the Church. But as C. S. Lewis observed, a price has to be paid for the millionaire's distinctive mistake:

> Picture how the camel feels, squeezed out
> In one long bloody thread from tail to snout.

'Social justice' is one crucial point at which the road forks, the Christian taking one direction and the secular humanist (accompanied by some 'liberation theologians') taking the other. Let us imagine some situation where weak people live in abject poverty, having had their blood sucked out by powerful people who now bathe in champagne. And of course, we don't need to *imagine* such a situation: it has always existed in countless places.

We can all agree that it's a bad situation. But how do we see its primary badness? In terms of the poor suffering? or in terms of the rich living in sin?

In the shadow of the Cross, can we see suffering as a simple evil?

We must live well, in justice and charity with all men, and part of what 'charity' means is a habitual and active concern for the sufferings of others.

That duty is part of being human. But 'being a

Catholic' is something further and (in that respect) subtly different. It involves a radical *metanoia*, a break with all 'natural' or sub-Christian ways of thinking and behaving, and notably with our very 'natural' instinct to see life in terms of satisfactions (which are good) *versus* sufferings (which are bad).

This instinct is what gives to the word 'Christian' the simply and insufficiently ethical meaning that I mentioned earlier. A selfish man (we naturally feel) is one who seeks only to maximise his own satisfactions and minimise his own sufferings: an unselfish and therefore good and therefore 'Christian' man (we naturally feel) is one who gives *exactly that same treatment* to other people and very little of it to himself.

The Cross of Christ by no means repeals that basic obligation, but it does change the subject, so to speak. It isn't about the elimination or even the reduction of suffering: it's about the redemptive *usefulness* of accepted suffering. This is one point at which 'being a Catholic' eases the despair of our raw human condition. We could always cope well enough with suffering: what drove us to despair was its pointlessness, its random distribution, its absurdity. Now, it becomes something which we can use.

This is just as well, since we're stuck with it—in the form of 'social injustice' (which will continue after any possible revolution) and in many other forms. It remains true, of course (to quote C. S. Lewis once again), that "a consistent practice of virtue by the human race even for ten years would fill the earth from pole to pole with peace, plenty, health, merriment, and heartsease, and that nothing else will." But I see no sign of that revolution coming to pass in my lifetime or in yours.

'Being a Catholic' isn't about the elimination of suffering; and in the same way, it isn't about 'being good', as the Anglo–American mind—in its instinctive Pelagianism—tends to suppose. It's about coping with the fact that we *aren't* good.

Charles Péguy once said that the sinner lies at the very heart of Christianity. If (like me) you're a sinner, take comfort from his words. They make us both into V.I.P.'s, people of central importance. It's for us that the whole operation exists.

One should not agonise too much over one's own sinfulness. This is real and must never be denied. But the thing to do is to repent each time and be absolved, and then to forget.

That possibility of being absolved is one prime element in 'being a Catholic', and why: it's also one of the factors that make 'the validity of priestly orders' into a matter of desperate practical urgency and no legalistic quibble. When Chesterton was asked why he became a Catholic, he said that he did so in order to get rid of his sins, and that's one good answer to the question. Mere confession, as to a friend or a psycho-analyst, can bring some psychological relief. But absolution is something else: you really can get your innocence back, you really can 'revert to childhood' in the only way that's possible or even desirable.

It's also a mistake to agonise too much over the sinfulness of mankind in general. Reading the newspapers, one can easily come to see all human life as a roaring cataract of wickedness, as though we were a race of demons. A little contact with your neighbours will rectify this illusion.

Not that there isn't any cataract of wickedness: there

is. But I sometimes suspect that in the sight of God, it may not be quite as bad as we suppose in our more sensitive moments. There's a great deal of madness going around, not always recognised as such, and it mitigates formal guilt. Is humanity perhaps less wicked than it seems, and a good deal crazier?

That is a good hypothesis to entertain when tempted to sit in judgment upon one's appalling neighbour, but a bad excuse to invoke in one's own case.

I once put it to a Cardinal: I suggested to him that the moral picture isn't as bad as it looks—that by reason of widespread sub-insanity, the sum of our formal guilt may be a great deal less than the torrential sum of our material guilt.

"I've always hoped and thought so", replied His Eminence; "If I didn't, I think I'd go out of my mind."

But we mustn't be casual about any sort of wickedness. Even where it does no visible harm at the time, it's what caused Mary's little boy to be skewered up there so bloodily, in the scorching sun and the swarming flies, while she looked on.

Her little boy? Every man, no matter how adult, remains forever a little boy in his mother's eyes.

How many million times, I wonder, has that hideous scene been represented in art? But seldom indeed has it been represented with very much realism.

Apart from the Catholic Church and Mussolini's Fascism, was there ever a movement or organisation which chose an instrument of torture and death to serve as its primary ikon or symbol or badge?

How could such an instrument ever be a sign of hope? You would expect it to throw people into despair, or to upset them and put them off at least.

I have heard of certain Catholic churches in which the

phoenix, rising mythologically from its own ashes, has replaced the crucifix. If there are such churches, one can only marvel at the stupendous talent which some people have for missing the point.

I once overheard a relevant exchange between a Priggish Young Man and an Intense Lady of Uncertain Age, both of them being Catholics. It ran as follows:

P.Y.M.: "Our Faith is all about suffering and death."

I.L.U.A.: "Oh, I do so disagree! For me, our Faith is all about *love*!"

P.Y.M.: "That's what I said."

It was indeed. Look at the two primary ikons or images of that Faith, and consider the relationship between them. The first—the one just mentioned— shows us a gaunt man being slowly tortured to death for no good reason, having first undergone a good working-over by the cops, and experiencing at the end (we are told) the ultimate in existential despair: the raw human condition at its worst. The other shows us a village girl with a baby on her knee—and, let us never forget, a baby born in circumstances that will undoubtedly have set the local busybodies a-gossiping. (Have you never lived in a village?)

Those are our two great images of love; and I am haunted by the irrelevance to both of the primary Buddhist ikon or image, which shows us a fat man sitting there timelessly, smiling secretly and serenely to himself. And people still say that the world's great religions, differing outwardly, are one at heart!

Yes, this Christian and Catholic Faith is most certainly about love. But it is so easy to overlook the crucifying complexity of that word: its affective and erotic senses are now so very dominant.

Jesus gave us a new commandment of love. But as I observed earlier, it *wasn't* new in the form "Love your neighbour as yourself": that was common to the ancient Hebrews and to all ethical systems everywhere. The new commandment was that his disciples should love one another *as he had loved them*; and that's a frighteningly different thing.

How *had* he loved them, after all?

He had called them away from perfectly innocent occupations (though the innocence of tax-collectors may be doubted), and also from that domesticity which his Church was to value so highly: he told them to turn their backs on all that, following him in a vocation which —as he said clearly—would involve hardship, conflict, rejection, seeming failure, and (for nearly all of them) violent death.

Was that a 'loving' way to treat people? Not as we most naturally understand the word. Where there's 'love', isn't there a desire to minimise suffering, not to pile it on gratuitously?

If you want to minimise suffering, there's one very obvious answer: minimise life.

That's the point at which, more acutely than elsewhere, I feel the difference between 'being a Catholic' and being something else. Nobody talks about 'minimising life' in any absolute sense. But a great many people now talk about the prevention or elimination of particular lives as a natural way of causing human suffering to be minimised; and there's a great deal of practical action in that sense, as we all know, not merely talk. Good Catholics oppose this, and rightly. But in my experience, many of them oppose it in defence of moral principle *alone*, with little or no reference to the underlying value-judgment, which is metaphysical or religious in nature. Where this is given insufficient emphasis, the moral principles in question are bound to seem arbitrary.

So let us turn to that value-judgment, which is the most basic of them all. I summed up the raw human condition by posing the relevant question: *Is it a good thing for us to exist and be alive as human beings?*

I also mentioned two plausible and popular answers to that question, while hinting at the possibility of a third.

The first answer is simply negative. Some people answer that question with a simple No. "Our existence in the body and in this world is endurable", they say, "but it is essentially illusory or evil or both." This value-judgment finds little formal expression in Western religion, but it is present and powerful—usually at some unconscious and inarticulate level—in a great many Western minds.

But the second answer is what mostly governs the post-Christian mind of our time. Countless people see it as the obvious answer, the only possible answer to that question, and are astonished to find any other answer taken seriously. "Well, it all depends, doesn't it? Human existence is certainly a good thing—that is, so long as certain minimal satisfactions and comforts are more or less guaranteed. But there's a point of adversity and suffering beyond which life simply isn't worth living. In certain circumstances, therefore, it's the kindest thing to prevent some potential human life or terminate some actual human life."

That Yes-and-No answer to my Great Question has its obvious attractions: it has a fine air of realism and common sense and also of compassion. Too many Catholics respond to it in moral terms alone, insisting stubbornly that contraception and sterilisation and abortion and euthanasia are sinful. They're perfectly right in saying so, of course, but this puts them in a tactically weak position, laying themselves open to an obvious rejoinder that is frequently heard in practice. "But isn't your God supposed to be a God of *love*? Aren't you people supposed to love your neighbour and all humanity? If the Pope insists on banning those things, he'll be adding enormously to the sum total of human misery. Doesn't he know that? Or doesn't he *care*?"

Thus we get a too-prevalent present-day notion of what 'being a Catholic' means. Above all else, it means being so utterly hung up on certain abstract principles of morality—mostly of sex-related morality—as to forget all compassion, all concern for the suffering of others.

If the Great Question were only capable of that Yes-and-No answer, that's exactly what it would mean.

But what if it were given a third and wholly positive answer?

'Being a Catholic': there are perspectives in which it can be seen as a Third Answer above all.

Human existence always involves suffering, and this can sometimes be bitter indeed, inescapable too: the life of man can certainly be "solitary, poor, nasty, brutish, and short". But with the first words of the Bible in mind, the first words of the Creeds as well, we believe in the goodness of the Creator; and we therefore see all human existence and in fact all 'being' as an absolute and unquantifiable good. Given this Third Answer, it makes no sense at all to speak of some point (of poverty or cancer or whatever) beyond which life simply isn't worth living.

This is the first principle (and paradox) of the Faith. It can be stated apothegmatically. It is not a good thing to be diseased and starving. But it is a good thing to *be*, even when diseased and starving.

A dear and terrible principle, and it's what divides the Church from the world most centrally—most *crucially*, I might say, remembering the etymology of that word. A more specific picture will throw it into sharper relief, and (if considered carefully) may help you to decide which side you're really on. Imagine a young girl who lives alone in a tar-paper shack, in some frightful shanty-town on the outskirts of a big city in—say—Latin America. She lives, of course, by prostitution; and eventually she has a baby whom she cannot feed. The big jets go fuming up from the airport nearby, tight-packed with steaks and martinis for the Beautiful People—that is, for you and me. But there's little for this girl to eat, so she has no milk; and in any case, the baby has inherited some of her diseases. So he looks out, briefly and with unfocussed eyes, upon God's world, and then he curls up and dies. His mother borrows a spade, buries him somewhere, and then goes back to work.

As you know, I am not being fanciful or morbid in outlining such a story: things of that sort happen all the time and in many places.

Was it a bad thing for that baby to die? It was an abomination, a blot on the entire human conscience: if you and I have any share in the responsibility for it, we must fear the Lord's anger.

But was it a bad thing for that baby to *live*?

Distinguish the two questions carefully, and think it over.

As a Catholic of this age and an argumentative one, I frequently find myself embroiled in controversy; and while this could be about a wide range of subjects, it tends—in practice—to be about a very few. Contraception, abortion, population-control, perhaps euthanasia: those are the things that people want to argue about when they find that you're a Catholic.

The first of those four questions is of course a matter of sexual morality, and the second is a matter of sex-related morality: the third concerns public policy in respect to the first and second. Only the fourth is devoid of any sexual or sex-related element, and in my experience, that's the one that gets the least controversial emphasis. I thus find it widely assumed, even by Catholics, that the great central issue between the Church and the world is moral and sexual in nature. On the one hand, there's some degree of permissive hedonism: on the other, there's an arduous but necessary sexual *askesis*.

Well, there clearly is an issue of that kind; and I do not wish to play down its importance, or to go along with those who recommend the easy way out. But as the debate proceeds, I am made more and more deeply aware of the underlying question, not moral in nature but theological and philosophical in nature, which is symbolised for us by that baby's brief existence. *Was* it a good thing for him to live? Countless people would say, instinctively and with some passion, that it was not.

In so doing, they take sides—perhaps quite unconsciously—in one of the ultimate of all possible debates. 'Being' and 'goodness' is where all philosophy has to begin: 'being' starts us off on ontology and epistemology and so forth, while 'goodness' starts us off on ethics, aesthetics, and of course religion. But how are those two rock-bottom concepts related?

As a Catholic, I see all being, human existence in particular, as an absolutely and unquantifiably good thing *per se*, though I know perfectly well that it's much more enjoyable in some circumstances than in others; and I don't see suffering as a simple negative, an unqualified evil. So believing, I confront people whose foreground preoccupation is with the rightness and even the necessity of contraception, abortion, population-control, and sometimes euthanasia, and who therefore challenge the Church about those moral questions. But that's on the surface. Their real challenge is made at that deeper level. For them, the goodness of human existence is not an absolute but depends upon circumstances, and can have a zero or negative value, as in the case of that poor little baby: they attach meaning to the concept of "a life that isn't worth living", whereas I do not. Hence, whatever they may think about sexual pleasures and sexual behaviour, they naturally favour those techniques and policies that will forestall or finish the life which— on their reckoning—is *not* going to be worth living. They see suffering as an unqualified evil about which nothing further can be said: it's there to be minimised, that's all, and if that means that we minimise existence— absolutely or relatively—why not?

Their outlook dominates the post-Christian societies of the present-day West, and it sometimes adopts particular disguises, of no obvious relevance to the four moral questions mentioned above. It is, for example, the outlook of those who say "Better dead than Red!" by way of justifying current preparations for nuclear war.

That catch-phrase is exactly parallel to the "Better dead than malformed!" by which so many abortions get justified: its implication is that if we suffer a Communist take-over, life will cease to be worth living. (Why is the former cry so very characteristic of the political Right, while the latter cry—identical in principle—is so very characteristic of the political Left? A good question.)

"Better to be than not to be, whatever the circumstances!" I nail that flag to the mast, that Third Answer to Hamlet: in the last analysis, it's what all those moral arguments are really about, and—for that matter—all the great arguments. It's *the* issue that divides today's Church from today's world: it's my central definition of what 'being a Catholic' is all about.

"But surely you ought to say 'Christian' there, rather than 'Catholic'? Protestants and others are just as deeply committed as you are to the idea of a loving Creator and of goodness in all being!"

I must proceed cautiously here: I have no wish to give unnecessary offence. Yes, all Christians are committed —in theory—to that twofold principle. But how deeply are non-Catholic Christians so committed in practice?

Very few of them come out squarely and speak in general terms of 'the life that isn't worth living' or 'the life that isn't worth preserving'. But how many of them bear consistently firm witness against all concrete implementation of that twofold and deeply un-Christian concept? Certain individuals undoubtedly do. But corporately, it's only the Catholic witness that's substantial. Some Catholics are weak in it, but only those who are otherwise in some degree of conflict with the tradition and teaching of their Church.

In this matter, it's essentially the Catholic Church

that's against the world, and the world is well aware of
the fact. Very powerful forces are at work, such as have
already caused contraception, abortion, and population-
control to seem wholly respectable things: euthanasia is
still groping its way towards respectability, but with
every hope of success. And those committed to such
causes know perfectly well that it's the Catholic Church,
not some generalised 'Christianity', that they're up
against.

For all practical purposes, we are just about the only
people who still believe in the inherent goodness of all
being.

"The inherent goodness of all being? But that takes us
back to the whole riddling problem of evil. How *can* this
hideously imperfect world be the handiwork of a loving
Creator? Or are you going to tell us that bad things don't
really exist at all? Was Auschwitz a kind of hallucination?
Or if it was real and therefore a part of total 'being', was
it somehow *good*?"

I'm glad you asked that question: it brings me to the
heart of my subject. Where it gets forgotten, there will
never be much point in 'being a Catholic'.

Earlier in this book, when I was talking about the raw
human condition, I outlined it briefly but as forcibly as I
could: I did my best to show that whatever we can
believe, we cannot believe consistently in a creating God
who is perfect in both love and power. The fact of
suffering, and of evil in general, means that the Christian
and Catholic option is ruled out by simple logic.

But is it?

Let us approach that question empirically and experientially in the first instance, considering the saints—that

is to say, the Catholics who took their Faith with total seriousness and commitment.

Imagine such a one as represented in an old painting. This shows us a gaunt and haggard man holding a crucifix—that is to say, an image of suffering and despair and death—and gazing upon it with burning intensity. By way of underlining the point, the picture may include a skull to remind us of our own death and the frustration of all temporal hope.

Now we shall know something about the particular life of this wholly generalised saint. When we turn to the books, we may find that he dedicated himself without reserve to relieving the sufferings of others: we may however find that he lived as a hermit, with practically no human contacts at all. He will certainly have lived penitentially, as though suffering on his own part were some kind of positive good, not simply an unavoidable evil to be endured with fortitude. Even that hermitage will have been no comfortable cop-out and retreat. While there, he will have suffered what some would call extremes of psychological stress: others, possibly more realistic, would describe this in terms of continual attack by demons. And if this holy man were martyred at the end, he will have greeted the experience with joy.

Yet the record shows that he *did* believe in a creating God who is perfect in both love and power, and all the more fervently by reason of this close and chosen involvement with suffering.

How are we to explain this recurring phenomenon? Psychologically?

Masochism is certainly not the answer: this saint got no sexual or other 'pleasure' from his sufferings. But with much less crudity, one might observe that a human being will often find it possible to believe contradictories by separating his mind into two halves, one believing this and the other believing that: an absurdity for the logician but a fact of experience for the psychologist. (And for the rest of us too. Listen carefully, and you'll find many a friend of yours expressing views that are logically incompatible with one another.)

But this saint is clearly not a case in point. It's all a unity for him: he loves God in and through his sufferings, he welcomes his sufferings precisely as a road to God.

The key to this enigma is in his hands. It's the crucifix that he's staring at. I called this "an image of suffering and despair and death", and there are many such images: our newspapers are full of them. But in this case, it's God who suffers and despairs and dies.

Never forget the further sense in which he does so in those newspaper-cases as well. The long passion of mankind is his Passion too.

That saint, in the picture, may or may not be a philosopher. Either way, cerebrally or instinctively, he will have by-passed the so-called 'problem of evil', recognising it as the pseudo-problem which it is. If it were a real problem, it would clearly be an insoluble one. Earlier on, when I tried to make it seem insoluble, I was cheating: I was breaking the rules that govern all strict reasoning in such matters. You may or may not have noticed me doing so.

This is a book about 'being a Catholic', not a philosophical essay on theodicy; so in this connection, I shall only throw out two small bones for the reader to chew upon in the philosopher's manner.

I offered the argument in two versions, and each

depended upon the coherence of a key sentence. In the first place, I represented a philosopher as saying "If God is a loving Father, as the Christians maintain, he will want to make his creatures perfectly happy": then, I represented a bereaved mother as asking, "Could God have prevented my baby from dying?" Each sentence appears to make perfectly coherent sense. Yet each contains a hidden contradiction and is strictly meaningless: neither can form part of a coherent argument.

Consider the first. In this life, we have no experience of 'perfect happiness'. We have moments of supreme bliss, but these are imperfect because temporary, even though we may not advert to their temporary nature at the time. But, while we do not know what the perfect happiness of a rational creature would *be like*, we can define the only thing that it could possibly *be*: it would be the free, total, unimpeded, and reciprocal gift of self to God and of God to self, the totality of what we mean (both ways) by 'the love of God' or by 'Heaven'. The closest thing to this in our present experience—though it isn't very close—is the free, total, unimpeded, and reciprocal gift of self (both ways) in marital love.

But all depends on that word 'free'. God can invite us to make that gift: he can help us to do so, by means of what theology calls 'grace'. But he cannot *cause* us to make it—not because his omnipotence fails at that point, bringing him up against something stronger than himself, but because the idea of him doing so is self-contradictory. A free gift that you're caused to make is not a *free* gift at all.

So if the word 'make' implies cause or coercion, God remains almighty without being able to 'make' us perfectly happy. He can invite us to happiness and smooth

the way before us, and in fact he does exactly that: he's
simply dying to make us happy. But in logic—not only
in theology—there's nothing else that he can do.

A dim reflection of this fact is visible in human
relationships. We must work for the happiness of our
nearest and dearest, and indeed of all mankind. But we
can never *cause* other people (or ourselves) to be happy.
Men are commonly stronger than women. But their
greater power does not mean that the quasi-Heaven of
marital bliss is attainable through rape.

Then, there's the paradoxical but crucial fact that
while we attribute 'omnipotence' to God, we also deny
him all 'potentiality'. In the Old Testament and the New
as well, we are positively encouraged to think and talk
about him in boldly analogical and anthropomorphic
language; and in that sort of language, we naturally talk
as though he lived in time, faced alternatives, and then
made choices between them, so proceeding from potency
to act. This is a practical necessity for much theology and
for the lower reaches of devotion too, though the great
mystics go beyond it: custom may blind us to the dangers
that arise when we try to syllogise in such language.

"Could God have prevented my baby from dying?"
It's wholly natural that the bereaved mother, in her
agony, should ask that question, and if we are holy and
humble enough, we may be able to offer an operationally
devout resolution of it. She isn't in a very philosophical
mood, after all. But later on, when her grief has subsided,
we may meet her when she *is* in a philosophical mood,
convinced that her tragedy refutes all Christian thinking
about God as though by logic. We shall then need to tell
her that if we are to be logical, we shall have to recognise
that earlier and agonised question of hers as strictly

meaningless. God is that of which it is ungrammatical
to speak except in the present indicative—and in the
extended or infinite present, not with reference to a
'now' which is distinct from his 'then' or his 'soon'.
To speak of what God 'could have' done is, in most
contexts, a lawful *façon de parler*. But one mustn't talk
like that when one is attempting to prove something
with the logician's sort of rigour.

Will these considerations comfort the bereaved mother,
or otherwise alleviate the long agony of mankind? No,
they will not, and I make no such claim for them. Their
sole function is that of indicating the lines on which one
logical-seeming obstacle to Christian belief can be by-
passed. In the extreme of agony, one cries out to God
(like Jesus) and may perhaps curse him (like Job): that's
very natural, and it's noteworthy that God didn't object
to Job's curses. The mistake comes in when we suppose
that we can thereby *prove* something bad about him.

We can't. Where the 'problem of evil' appears to do
so, language has been misused at some point. In his faith
and life, that pictured saint of mine—or any other
Christian—is not primarily being logical. But there is no
point at which he needs to be illogical.

But 'being a Catholic' isn't something that comes
naturally to us. We belong to an enquiring species, and
we naturally see things in terms of question-and-answer:
we live in a highly technological age, and we naturally
see things technologically, in terms of problem-and-
solution. (A problem is something that we hope to solve
by means of a technique: a technique is something that
we use for solving problems, whether discursive or
practical.)

Hence our natural instinct to see evil also as a 'problem', one that we might hope to solve by some intellectual or other technique. But it isn't that kind of thing at all: if we treat it as though it were, it turns out to be a pseudo-problem. It's a *mystery*; and I suppose that the writers of detective-stories must carry some part of the blame for the fact that most people see that word as more or less synonymous with 'problem'. Sherlock Holmes and Lord Peter Wimsey were always solving mysteries.

But they weren't. A problem is something that we may perhaps solve by means of a technique: a mystery is something that we come to understand by means of contemplation.

That's why my generalised saint was staring at a crucifix. It's by contemplating the Cross of Christ that we come to understand the *mysterium iniquitatis*.

One crude way of stating what we then come to understand: we see God at the receiving end of all the world's grief and misery, not at the originating and responsible end.

One further fruit of our contemplation (not the most important) will be a deeper understanding of the radical difference between three things which are commonly confused: pain, evil, and suffering.

They are not at all the same thing. Pain is a neurological event and—biologically speaking—a useful one: it is one of the body's defence-mechanisms. Evil is strictly a moral thing. All being, as such, is good; but a rational creature with free will can turn away from God and so reject the ground or basis of his own being and move—asymptotically, as it were—towards non-existence. His decision to do so is the only thing (or un-thing) that can be called 'evil' in any absolute sense.

But suffering is something else. We naturally think of it in terms of *very great* suffering, of cancer or bereavement, and we forget how wide and simple a concept it is. To suffer is to have anything—great or small—otherwise than as you wish or will or want it to be. If your self-will is powerful and untamed, you will 'suffer' horribly when you miss a train or run out of cigarettes: if your self-will is wholly conformed to the will of God, as manifested in the circumstances of the moment, you can undergo extremes of physical pain without 'suffering' at all. Hence the joy of the martyrs: hence the serenity of an agonising but saintly death-bed.

We must therefore speak very cautiously about animal sufferings. It is clear that pain, as a neurological event, takes place in animal bodies. But is it there accompanied (as it is in us) by self-will, by a desire that things should be different? If it is, we shall have to attribute free will to the animals; and while they certainly do appear to 'choose', we shall then be on philosophically dangerous ground. But if they have no free will and therefore no self-will, they cannot—strictly speaking—be said to 'suffer'. (But it would be unwise and wrong to treat them accordingly, our pets and our beasts of burden especially, since they are such very powerful metaphors for humanity.)

A further and most central inference needs careful treatment. Christians have always made the Passion of Christ into an object of contemplation and (among other things) of simple human compassion: the Son of God suffered and died for us, and we desire to suffer and die with him, which is what 'compassion' or 'sympathy' means. (Some devotional language suggests that we actually *desire* suffering and death, or that we ought to do so, and I certainly can't do that. But we're going to get sufferings and death anyway, and any one of us can desire them to be conformed and assimilated to his.)

Now it's clear that in every ordinary sense, Jesus 'suffered' to an extreme degree. Countless other men have been tortured to death, of course, some of them by crucifixion, and their 'pain'—in the strictly neurological sense—may often have equalled his. But we must assume that his Godhead gave it a further and unique dimension, though we cannot imagine this and should probably not try.

Then there was clearly a question of self-will. Nobody wants to be flogged and crucified, and Gethsemane shows us that the Monothelites were wrong, that there was a real conflict of will between Jesus as man and Jesus as God, and perhaps between the Son and the Father—a conflict that was fully resolved. ("From all eternity, or at some point within those few hours?" If our minds were not trapped within space and time, we would probably see that as an unreal distinction.)

But since that conflict was fully resolved, there has to be a sense—if you can understand it, you can understand all things—in which the crucified Lord didn't want things to be different and was thus (dare I say it?) not 'suffering' at all.

No: I shrink back from that rashness. It might be better to say that while the Cross shows us the extreme of suffering and despair and death, it shows us that extreme transformed. It is a picture of Good Friday, but

Easter Sunday is already there. This is why so many artists and sculptors have shown us a Christ who is already crowned in kingly majesty while in the very act of being crucified. *Regnabit a ligno Deus*: his defeat isn't just followed by a victory, it *is* a victory.

"But how can it be a *complete* victory? It still leaves Auschwitz on the record! That wasn't just a hallucination, you know! Or can God somehow cause the bad things never to have happened at all? And what about the eternal torments of the damned?"

'Auschwitz' may certainly stand as a convenient shorthand term for the whole vast totality of human wickedness and human suffering. (We must remember, of course, that human suffering is not always caused by human wickedness, or not in any direct fashion that we can perceive.)

Well, *can* Christ's victory cause Auschwitz never to have happened at all? Can God undo the past?

It's our first instinct to reply to both questions with a straightforward common-sense No. The ugly past actually happened. We may move on to something very much better. But it still remains true that while the ugly past was going on, it actually was going on. Nothing can alter that: the real can never turn out not to have been real after all. Auschwitz has to remain on the record forever.

Yet a fairly common experience shows us that this can't be the whole story. We have all lived through sufferings that seemed overwhelming but eventually passed away. We don't here need to speak of anything as extreme as Auschwitz: you had a toothache, let us say, and it made your life a misery while it lasted. But with the dentist's help, it came to an end. It was perfectly real at the time: it has now stopped being real, though we must still say that it *was* real.

But now consider the different experience of waking up from a nightmare, during which horrors and demons tore your soul to pieces. A crucial distinction becomes obvious at once. There has to be some sense—let the philosophers get to work on it!—in which the horrors and demons were 'real': you experienced them directly, if only in the phantasmal experience of sleep, which is why you woke up in a muck of sweat and terror. But as you struggled back into full consciousness, you didn't just realise that they had ceased to be real as that tooth-ache did: there is a further sense—let the philosophers get to work on it!—in which you then realised that they never had been real at all.

Common experience thus casts some light upon what might otherwise seem an impenetrable mystery, even an absurdity. "Auschwitz never really happened." So long as our conceptual and verbal systems are governed by the limitations of space and time, that must always remain a simple falsehood. But only for so long: we shall wake up one day.

The eternal torments of the damned? By illustrating the justice of God, do they contribute to the joys of the saved? Some terrible people have said so. But I suspect them of a category-mistake rather than of heartlessness: once again, they have been fooled by the limitations of spatio-temporal thinking.

Let us imagine some castle in the good old days. Upstairs, the great hall is suffused with light and music, and the Beautiful People are carousing over the venison and the wine. They are enjoying themselves enormously —and all the more keenly, perhaps, because of what they know to be happening down below, where foul wretches are being tortured in hideous dungeons. "Better you than me!" they think, complacently; and they go on to reflect on the great King's justice, which rewards the good and punishes the wicked so admirably.

If the saved and the damned were really like that, co-existing within the same spatio-temporal framework, Hell and not Heaven would have won: the *schadenfreude* of the saved would be demonic. But do they so co-exist? Or have the damned, in their refusal of Being, stampeded off asymptotically into the non-framework of the never-really-was?

We can't help playing this sterile game of trying to imagine the unimaginable. But two things are (I think) clear. One is that the justice of God is both beautiful and terrifying. It's there in the Book: "Ask and you shall receive." Then, consider the hall and the dungeons in that great castle and look at the nearest crucifix. If we are to entertain such a picture at all, our present limitations mean that we shall have to list God among the wretches who are being tortured down below. Upstairs, among the Beautiful People, it's Satan who's presiding, King of Power and Pride. That's a good image to bear in mind when you want to understand the things you read about in the newspapers.

Power? No, he's already been defeated in battle. That's what the Paschal liturgy is all about.

'Being a Catholic': what does it mean?

One good answer: a Catholic is one who stands in contemplation, with Mary and John, by the Cross of

Christ, finding there the one-and-only remedy for the despair of our raw human condition, generally and in this age of possibly exceptional despair.

But 'contemplation' is a tricky word: it can easily suggest distance, detachment, non-involvement, a mere thinking-about. The Catholic identity as there described might therefore be seen as a kind of pretence, an imaginative exercise at the best. The Crucifixion happened a long time ago, after all, and in a remote country: we can think about it, but we cannot really "stand by the Cross of Christ", any more than we can go back to any other moment and event in history.

Of course we can't—not if the materialists are right, that is, and if space and time are the absolutes that we most naturally take them to be. But we, living after Einstein, have a certain advantage here, one that was denied to our forefathers: we are less likely to suppose that time and space *are* absolutes. There are further scientific developments—in sub-atomic physics, for example—that now make it hard to sustain the old Victorian confidence in strictly deterministic materialism.

And what if the Catholic Faith turned out to be true? and, in particular, the eucharistic theology of such writers as de la Taille?

Let us suppose that by magic, a devout Christian found it possible to borrow Wells's Time Machine and so go pedalling back, on that curious quasi-bicycle with its quartz rods, until he found himself in New Testament times: let us suppose that he then made the geographical journey as well, and so was present at the Last Supper and the Crucifixion too.

Those events, *as thus experienced by him*, would be very unlike what a present-day Catholic lives through during Sunday Mass, that fidgety hour in a draughty church of his own suburb. But the realities of time and space and sacrament mean that they would be the same thing in fact—not two obviously similar things, not two symbolically related things, but the *same* thing. Given the two options—Time Machine or Sunday Mass—there would be nothing to choose between them.

But only the genuine Mass constitutes this journey and miracle; and this gives a further explanation of the fuss that Catholics make about 'validity', in the priest's orders and in the rite. If we were simply talking about an *imaginative* journey back to the Upper Room and Calvary, about shared experience in a commemorative meal, all that would be fuss of the most unnecessary and legalistic kind. But before embarking on a real journey, you need to be very sure that your Time Machine is in good working order: you need to fuss over its subtleties and precisions, you need to study the Operating Instructions in a spirit of great punctiliousness, checking everything, as an airline pilot does before take-off.

So—in fact, though not in directly apprehended fact—a Catholic is one who is present at the Last Supper and who stands, with Mary and John, at the foot of the Cross.

He may do well to remember that Peter was present at the first occasion but not at the second. The Papacy is of crucial importance for the integrity of the Faith and the life of the Church. But together with all the rest of the ecclesiastical structure, it is ancillary in function and a temporary thing. When we reach the heart of the matter, it falls away—rather as that supporting and sustaining gantry falls away from a space-rocket at the time of blast-off. Only love remains.

Looking back at the raw human condition, Neolithic or modern, I tend to see 'being a Catholic'—standing by the Cross—in terms of three perennial surprises. Life does have a point and purpose and meaning, after all: he became one of us, he is ours, we are his. We can believe in the benevolence of the almighty Creator and the goodness of all being, after all: from being a meaningless evil, suffering has been transformed into a divine thing. And we can *thank* God adequately, after all.

The first two of those surprises are concerned with the awfulness of life, but the third is concerned with the goodness and splendour of life—in itself, and in its Christian transformation (*mirabiliter condidisti et mirabilius reformasti*). Would it be a confession or a boast if I said that this is the one that matters most to me?

"Why be a Roman Catholic, as against all other versions of Christianity? Why go to Mass, when there are so many other ways of building community and fellowship, of honouring the Lord by a commemorative meal in common?"

The Mass does build community and fellowship, it is a commemorative meal in common and one that honours the Lord: it is also our 'real presence' in the Upper Room and at Calvary. But I think I value it most—the Mass, and the 'Catholicism' or integral discipleship that makes it available to me—as the thank-offering which it declares itself to be, as the only possible way of thanking God *sufficiently*.

That's a primary duty, otherwise incapable of performance. There's any amount of debate about morality, about good and bad behaviour, but ingratitude is universally recognised as a fault and a thoroughly nasty one, even as between human beings. You don't find even the most innovative moral theorists justifying the ungrateful man.

When Sunday comes or some other day of obligation, I can choose to go to Mass. I can also choose not to; and since that hour in an ugly church seldom offers me very much in the way of felt spiritual exaltation, I might well consider the time better spent elsewhere. But the decision not to go—on those appointed days at least— would be the most ungrateful decision of which I am capable.

The same principle might be expressed more positively, though on lines that would seem cryptic if one didn't know the background doctrine. Why go to Mass? "In order to add my voice to the *Amen* at the end of the Canon."

A partial answer, but a good one even so.

The Cross is a serious thing to stand by, and 'a Catholic' is—or should be—a serious and even a frightening thing to be. The sea is never to be taken lightly, least of all when it's as strange and divine as this one.

It's with good cause that the Church speaks traditionally in terms of front-line seriousness, offering Good News indeed, but on sobering terms. "She will permit no comforts", said Belloc; "the cry of the martyrs is in her far voice; her eyes that see beyond the world present us heaven and hell to the confusion of our human reconciliations, our happy blending of good and evil things. By the Lord! I begin to think this intimate religion . . . is as tragic as first love, and drags us out into the void away from our dear homes."

The story has an ending for which 'happy' is a wildly insufficient word, as is 'goodness' when applied to God: 'being a Catholic' is a matter of hope and joy, even sometimes of exhilaration, but also—at this stage in our journey—of a certain awed seriousness. I have asked this question before and I will ask it again: why do our Bishops—men of God's blood and the martyrs' agony —grin like politicians when being photographed, as though the whole thing were some footling joke?

The Gospel is Good News, but *solemnly* good, and in some ways alarmingly so. Dietrich von Hildebrand was a great philosopher; and just before he died, I happened to observe him at the moment of Communion, of eating God. I wouldn't have thought it possible that human features could convey, at one and the same moment, such extremes of love and of terror.

Most of us contrive to be Catholics for many years, perhaps throughout life, without his sort of understanding —without the terror, therefore, but (all too probably) without the love as well. That shattering consummation can then come to seem like a routine.

The great thing is that there's hope for us bad Catholics, not only for the saints that you and I so obviously aren't. What despair we'd be in if we were to be judged on our strict merits! But we aren't; so we plod along, weakly and badly, distracted by a thousand trifles, "still nursing the unconquerable hope" in this Church of sinners, entitled to do so unless we refuse to stand by the Cross when summoned.

As so often, common or public opinion hit upon the central point, the heart of the matter, without really seeing what it was. It isn't sufficient to see 'being a Catholic' in terms of going to Mass alone. But it's a good beginning.

Christ—as found in the Mass, and in his Church and Faith generally and also in our neighbour—is of supreme relevance to our raw human condition, and will only seem irrelevant if, in the fuss and folly of our daily preoccupations, we forget what that condition is. It's therefore a good thing to read the great pessimists and despairers from time to time: Lucretius, Hardy, Sartre. By keeping alive our sense of the problem, they help us to remember the point of the solution.

Here, in this strange divine sea of our baptism, we are still alienated and in exile but are on our way home; we cannot yet see the satisfaction of our deepest longings, but we do know where to look; we are still sinners, but we can get our innocence back; we are still going to suffer, but not pointlessly or absurdly; we are still going to 'die', but not in the old sense, not permanently. The meaning and point and purpose of life has come upon us and taken us over: we are free!

Or, rather, we have been freed. The door of our jailhouse or prison camp has been blasted open. But we still find it a tricky and painful and sometimes tedious business, picking our way through the splinters and rubble of this too-familiar human world for what seems an interminable lifetime.

We are committed, in fact, to a 'long march', rather like that of the Mormons or the Chinese Communists, although to a very different sort of destination. It can be wearisome. I would like to say that 'being a Catholic' was something that I experienced, from day to day, as the poetic exaltation which the words of my title might suggest. It is, but only sometimes, and not always (I suspect) at my spiritually best moments. There is much to suggest that in every such visionary sense, our Church and Faith is most clearly visible from the outside, as by Helen Waddell when she called it a "strange divine sea". The sea is romance for the poet and the holidaymaker, but work and routine for the sailorman.

One can become terribly bored with 'being a Catholic', and most easily—in my case at least—where there's infection by the grey mould of neo-Modernism. This does something which the Protestant Reformers never achieved. It makes this tremendous thing seem not evil but commonplace: it reduces our strange divine sea into just another human puddle.

We have to co-exist with that, and to suffer much else as well. We were never promised an easy and enjoyable ride: all the spiritual writers agree that while there would be moments of vision and sweetness and 'consolation', these would come mostly in the early stages of the journey and should not be taken too seriously. We should be grateful for them as for confectionery: they would not be food. Our best moments would come unnoticed when—finding the drudge and tedium almost unendurable—we still marched on in the heat and the dust and the flies.

I see the needed fidelity in terms of the Third Answer above all—in terms of the goodness of all being, so hard to perceive directly, so easy to apprehend through the difficult Cross, and with Eucharistic and other gratitude as the primary business of life. (And do I always behave accordingly? No, I can snivel and complain as easily as you can, I can set myself up as God and then curse the world because it has more sense than to worship me. But then, I'm only trying to write a book about 'being a Catholic', not about 'being a saint' or even 'being reasonably good'. This is a Church of sinners: that's why I feel at home in it.)

'Being a Catholic': it isn't the same thing as being good, and it certainly isn't a way of causing daily life to *seem* strange and divine and oceanic or otherwise transformed and different. It's a way of making it *be* transformed and different, sins and all; so you have to believe in the difference between 'being' and 'seeming', you have to care about that philosophical difference. I suspect that for a great many people in this sceptical age, the practical problem lies exactly there; which may be why God chose a philosopher to succeed Pope John Paul I.

A long march, largely in the dark. But the undeserved moments of vision and astonishment do come. From time to time and perhaps briefly—if you bear the Third Answer steadily in mind—you suddenly see the point of all the fuss, the apparent legalism, the drudge and routine. Our remade condition is far better than we suppose. We haven't been forgotten, we aren't alone: *Maria undique, et undique caelum*.